finding peace

Letting Go and Liking It

Paula Peisner Coxe

SOURCEBOOKS, INC.®
NAPERVILLE, ILLINOIS

Published by Sourcebooks, Inc.
P.O. Box 4410, Naperville, Illinois 60567-4410
(630) 961-3900
FAX: (630) 961-2168
www.sourcebooks.com

Library of Congress Cataloging-in-Publication Data
Coxe, Paula Peisner
  Finding peace : letting go and liking it / by Paula Peisner
Coxe.— 3rd ed..
    p. cm.
  ISBN 1-4022-0249-0 (alk. paper)
  1. Peace of mind. I. Title.
BF637.P3P46 2004
170'.44—dc22

                                        2004001929

Printed and bound in the United States of America
VP 10 9 8 7 6 5 4

For my daughters,
Samantha and Francesca,
may peace be your constant companion
as you journey through life—
you are my blessings.

Table of Contents

Introduction 1

The You of Yesterday 19
   Childhood 25
   Parents 33
   Mistakes 43
   Forgiveness 49
   Acceptance 55
   Purpose 61
   Understanding 67
   Pride 73
   Emotions 79
   Obstacles 85
   Baggage 91
   Fear 97

The You of Today .103
   Permission 107
   Attitude 113
   Silence 123
   Tolerance 129
   The Present 137
   Happiness 143
   Pain 151
   Criticism 157
   Serenity 163
   Satisfaction 169
   Love 175
   Friendship 181
   Comparisons 187

Doubt 193
Reality 201
Health 209
Spirit 215
Mind 221
Body 227
Time 233
Life 239
Security 245
Crisis 251
Rights 257

The You of Tomorrow 263
Making Room 269
Hope 275
Growth 281
Change 285
Destiny 289
Choice 293
Vision 299
Reason 303
Optimism 307
Empowerment 311
Confidence 317
Knowing 323
Compassion 327
Sharing 333
Generosity 339

Some Final Thoughts on Peace 343
About the Author 344

Introduction

Quieting the noise in your mind. Accepting yourself
and your life for what it is. Trusting more and worrying less. Comparing yourself to no one. Loving
yourself. Fearing nothing. Forgiving past pain.
Letting your losses build, not break you. To achieve
this state of being is to reach a place where few reside
and many seek—a place called peace of mind.

It's the uncommon ability to deal with the
world, your life, and the people in it with serenity and confidence. Occupied less with the need
to control and more with the wish to accept, less
with the longing to hold on and more with the
need to let go, you begin to trust that all things
happen for a reason, whether you know it at the
time or not. You realize that all mistakes are lessons to be learned and that your pain in times of
loss helps you to grow.

Loss softens the heart.

Touching all of our lives at one time or another, true and deep loss, the kind that tears your insides open and leaves you dry and unable to cry anymore, is, unfortunately, an inevitable part of life. Loss spares no one. Loss makes you human. Only by walking this path of pain, coupled with the passage of time, will pain make way for peace of mind. As you walk your private path of pain, seek faith as your companion to comfort and clear the way for peace of mind.

Finding peace is willingly and joyfully letting go of the need to hold on, forgiving to allow forgetting, and living in the present, not the pain of the past. Peace of mind reflects coming to terms with all that you've been, all that you are, and all that you will become. The operative word here is *being*, not *doing* or *having*. A state of mind harbors peace—who we are, not what we do, nor what we have.

Peace of mind comes over time and is largely based on letting go of past pains, hurts, anger, and guilt while surrendering yourself to live fully and lovingly in the present with faith in yourself and in God above.

There has been so much that has happened in your life that you carry with you today—all the events of your child, teen, and young adult years that have tested your faith and the very fiber of your being. Sometimes the past clouds the present and prevents you from seeing tomorrow. Your pain, fears, and worries create noise in your mind and doubt in your heart.

You lose precious moments in time when you look backwards too long and wonder "Why?"

Of course, it is important to come to terms with yourself and your life by first contemplating what was—your past—and the lasting effects of why things happened. Then you can better deal with the present and plan for the future. But, too often, you lose yourself in the past at the expense of doing what you need to do today and miss the joys of the moment. This book deals with ways to find peace of mind through working with the three main time components of your life:

The You of Yesterday: This is the hurt and pain of old memories that cast a cloud over making the most of your life today.

The You of Today: This is what is, what you are today, and how fully living your life in the present allows true personal growth and peace of mind the room to grow. This is my primary focus, for the past is gone and the future is yet to be.

The You of Tomorrow: This is the hopeful, dreaming you—that part of you that looks at what may be and reaches for the stars.

Within each of these phases of life, this book will explore aspects of the way you think and feel and how you treat yourself and others. Using the carefully crafted thoughts and suggestions con-tained in the following pages, you have the opportunity to contemplate how you let the past influence you, how you live your life today, and how faith and hope will move you forward on the path to greater inner peace.

Now is the time to give yourself the greatest gift of all—the peace of mind to let go of the past, live in the present, and let tomorrow be. Even if you feel pretty good and life is not so bad for you, there is always room to grow and deepen your sense of inner satisfaction and personal peace.

I hope this book serves as a source of inspira-tion for you.

Ten years have passed since I first wrote *Finding Peace—Letting Go and Liking It.* Much has happened and I am still learning and growing.

I liken this book to a heartbeat. *Finding Peace* has one and I am thankful. My heart has been touched by the beautiful letters that I have received over the years from readers who have found grains of truth in this book and been comforted through their difficult days.

To update *Finding Peace*, I sat down at my kitchen table, a more mature and experienced woman than the one who originally penned these words. On this ordinary morning, I had an extraordinary thought.

Peace needs a foundation on which it can be built.

I have come to learn that there are certain essential pillars that nourish the spirit and fuel personal growth. Your ability to achieve personal growth is only as strong as your foundation. Similarly, in your search for peace of mind, you will only be as successful as the strength of your foundation—the basic belief system through which you view yourself and others.

While the book's format remains unchanged— Yesterday, Today, and Tomorrow— I have added new ideas in each chapter and have woven a common thread through them all—the concept of the four pillars. These pillars construct the foundation of your spiritual journey and your search for peace:

- Faith
- Other-directedness
- Balance
- Loss

Contemplate the strength of these four pillars in your life as you set out on your personal exploration:

Faith—Essential to your emotional and spiritual growth is believing in God, in a force greater than that which we see in the material world, that which only exists in eternity, that which knows all, sees all, forgives all, and loves all. Whether you subscribe to Christianity, Judaism, Buddhism, Hinduism, or any other religion, having faith forms a strong foundation upon which peace of mind can flourish. This faith allows you to surrender yourself, find lasting comfort and support during turbulent times, and find the peace of mind you seek. Because of my background and life experiences, I will be referring to God, prayer, and the Bible throughout this book. It is my hope that if this does not fit in with your own religious beliefs and practices, you will still be able to translate and apply these tips to the language of your faith.

Other-directedness—If we would only live our lives by uttering four simple words—"How can I help?"—we would reach out to others and find the blessed satisfaction that comes with demonstrating compassion, empathy, understanding, love, and patience. Do good and you will do well. It's too easy to stay stuck on yourself and react to others through your own reflection, as though you have a perpetual mirror in front of you. It's too easy to be self-absorbed by looking inward at your own private fears and concerns and striving to achieve your personal goals and objectives of status, power, and position. It's too easy to judge others and look at what they may have done to you and not reach out to them to understand their needs and worries. Through living an other-directed life, you demonstrate that in giving, you receive and in selflessness, you soar.

Balance—Too many demands, responsibilities, and things out of your control pull at you every day. Sometimes, in my own private tug-of-war, I feel like Gumby, that character made of clay who can stretch until his skin becomes paper thin. Peace can only exist where you give it room to grow. An essential way to make room for peace is to strive to keep a sense of balance in life, to constantly seek to do that which is important, to be flexible and bend—not break—when outside forces try to move you off your mark, to be well-rounded and not excessively dependent on one aspect of life to the detriment of others, and to learn to let the noise and uncontrollable events that will surely happen slide off your back. Balance is about harmony—an evenness, a steadiness, and an equilibrium in all that you do. Understanding your purpose in life—why you are here on this earth—is essential to finding balance and focusing on the important rather than the unimportant, the essential, not the expedient.

Loss—You are born with nothing and leave this world with nothing. In this regard, that which you possess is, in fact, borrowed. In the deepest sense, you cannot lose that which is not yours. This, however, is hard to understand in everyday life when you experience a wide range of emotions such as hurt, pain, anger, and confusion. Many of these sensations are associated with feeling some kind of loss. Real or imagined, loss comes in many shapes and colors: illness, death, unemployment, divorce, break-ups, bankruptcy, aging, dependency, diminished power or position, and financial difficulties. Accepting loss as a necessary part of life, as sure to happen as day turns to night, is essential to your search for peace. Loss knows no boundaries. It touches everyone's lives. And only through knowing what it means to lose do you grow and become a better human being.

Take a few moments before continuing on and consider how wholeheartedly you believe these four affirmations:

Faith: I believe in God and pray that Thy will be done.

Other-directedness: I seek to understand rather than be understood and ask, "How can I help?" with open heart and mind.

Balance: I balance the needs of my mind, body, and spirit as I fulfill my purpose in life by watching my priorities and following my heart.

Loss: I have experienced loss in many ways and my soul is richer, my mind is wiser, and my heart is softer for having done so.

These four pillars form the foundation for gaining a greater sense of inner peace. Please keep them in mind as you begin reading this book.

For this third edition, I reread this book with an eye toward updating its contents. Although the book was first published a decade ago, I discovered that what I said back then still holds true. However, I have woven in new insights and prescriptive ideas for you to consider in your self-discovery. The end of each chapter now offers Reflecting on My Finding Peace, Private Point to Consider, and Question to Myself. The purpose is to serve as a daily reminder or diary of sorts to use with as you wish.

The past five years have brought many unexpected changes to my life. I all too well understand that peace is a process, a journey of the heart which I, too, continue to work at every day. I work at making sense of nonsense that comes my way. I try to numb the pain of disappointments and unexpected turns in the road. I work at making peace a part of my everyday life. Reminding myself that peace is a process, not an end.

By picking up this book, you have said that you are interested in expanding your horizons, in going beyond ordinary life, as happy and safe as it may be. You are saying that who you are today is not enough. You may be thankful that you have your health, a good job, and a loving family, yet peace eludes you. You may worry and compare yourself to others more than you'd like. You may wish things were somehow different and find yourself saying "If only I had this" or "If only I was that." You may feel battered by the losses you've suffered and want to get up, make sense of it all, and move on. The one thing each of you have in common is the need to reach higher, to get to a better place in your life, a happier time.

Peace brings clarity. With peace, gaining a more balanced view of life unfolds. You see what's important and what's not. People, events, and experiences come into finer focus and become clearer. Often when we communicate, we psychologically place a mirror in front of ourselves. We filter comments by their reflection upon us and by how we feel without taking into account that what the other person is saying or doing may have nothing to do with us. How often have you reacted to someone's comments with "I didn't do anything," or thought "She probably thinks I'm an idiot"?

Instead, with inner peace you have the opportunity to react from a base of confidence, security, and love. You can say "I'm sorry that you're upset. How can I help?" or "I understand. You must feel pretty bad about it." This is one example of how finding inner peace will help you gain the strength and confidence you need to not let bad times get the best of you. Inner peace will allow you to look toward yourself and others with compassion, acceptance, and forgiveness—letting go and liking it

Remember, it's only human to err, but divine to forgive.

While reading this book, keep in mind that the best results for lasting change will come to those who *make a commitment to grow*. Stagnation stymies peace. You have to evolve constantly and change to make room for spiritual growth. Reading, in and of itself, is not enough. It is the first part. The second part of the process of finding peace of mind is to do something about it—to breathe life into words on a page. Behavior and actions are the only evidence of growth, that you are reaching for the stars to be all you can be. I invite you to use the diary section of each chapter to privately write down your thoughts, feelings, and what you will do to make peace of mind a priority in your life.

Take one day at a time. Step by step, you will make the journey when you are ready. Give yourself room for error, to be human, to make mistakes, and to have feelings you aren't proud of. Give yourself the time to learn and grow. Think of the words on these pages as water feeding the seeds of change that exist within. Intended to stimulate personal reflection and contemplation, the thoughts and words in this book are intended to *ask you to ask more of yourself.*

To walk this path, you have to believe. Believe that you have a purpose on this earth and that everything happens for a reason. Maybe you don't understand it now, but it will soon become clear.

Now, let's start the walk.

Peace only knows stillness, a sense of oneness with the world around you. To begin the process, why not take some time to be still, to quiet the noise in your mind? Set aside about thirty minutes. Go to a relaxing place where you feel you can think without interruption or worry. Close your eyes and simply be still. Do nothing. Relax. Stretch the muscles in your neck and back. Get comfortable. You may find this difficult to do and itch to get up and run an errand, make a phone call, or go on the Internet. Restrain yourself from the doer and busy bee inside and just *be*. Now it is time to quiet your mind, relax your body, and make sense of all the nonsense out there. To do so, you need desire, discipline, commitment, and dedication. Peace of mind demands no less.

I was blessed to have a very wise and loving uncle in my childhood. My uncle David, a professor, sociologist, and humanitarian who lived most of his life in Montreal, wrote "Words to Remember," which serve to inspire us as a reminder to live each day generously, selflessly, and honestly on our path to inner peace:

Words to Remember

The six most important words are, "I admit I made a mistake."

The five most important words are, "You did a good job."

The four most important words are, "What is your opinion?"

The three most important words are, "If you please?"

The two most important words are, "Thank you."

The least important word is, "I."

My hope is that by reading this book and applying it to your life, you will understand that everything happens for a reason that becomes clear over time. My prayer is that you follow your heart when you hear its beat and, in stillness, find true comfort and peace of mind.

Give yourself this gift.

And thank you for taking the time to let this book touch your life.

—Paula Coxe

January 2004

The You of Yesterday

Learning from your mistakes. Picking yourself up from defeat. Loving and losing. Crying and laughing. In large part, the very person you are today is shaped by the experiences of your past— the good and the not-so-good. From the time of infancy, your subconscious mind has recorded the feelings and emotions, the pains and joys of childhood. For many of us, it is the cuts and bruises that leave tender imprints on our hearts.

Perhaps as a small child you were told that you weren't good enough, or that you should be more like your brother, sister, or even the neighbor's child. No doubt these comments, whether intentionally or not, hurt—particularly if they came from your parents, the very ones who protect and guide you. An indelible scar remains, one that is only erased over time by forgiveness and under-standing—the fruits of personal growth in the present.

Peace of mind eludes those who seek external rewards. Most of us were told to "be a nice girl" and "be good." We attempt in vain to please, look for control, fear abandonment, seek approval, and judge others. All of these ways of dealing with people and the world around us harden our hearts and close our minds.

When we try too hard to be perfect, we let ourselves down. When we expect others to be perfect, we let them down and, at the same time, set ourselves up for disappointment.

Having said this, now what can you do to change it?

Open your heart.

Simple to say and difficult to do, opening your heart starts by shining an unfiltered light on the self-perpetuating patterns you carry with you, day in and day out. You cannot understand what you do not want to see. Seek to see first, then understand. Once you have achieved understanding, forgiveness follows closely. And forgiveness clears the path to peace of mind.

To shed light on your own particular behavior patterns, contemplate these three questions:

1. **Do you look to others for validation and approval?**
   You feel you are only as good as someone says you are. You need external gratification to be motivated and satisfied. You lose your own desires in favor of pleasing others. You act with the objective of wanting to be liked instead of doing what is right and true to your inner self.

2. **Do you expect that others will act as you want?**
   You seek to control and mold outcomes to your expectations instead of surrendering to the situation and being

21

flexible in meeting the needs of others. You are too quick to pass judgment. You have unrealistic expectations. You end up easily disappointed because others will not do what you want.

3. **Do you try to be someone you're not?** You avoid the depths of true self-discovery and walk through life satisfying the needs of others instead of listening to your inner voice and facing your fears to be all that you can be.

The answers you form lay the foundation for the work ahead. It's all about questioning your assumptions and dealing with feelings you hide deep inside. It's about letting go of the need to hold on to unhelpful habits and ways of looking at yourself. Our lives too often sound like a one-note samba—"If only…": "If only I had more money," "If only I was more successful," "If only I was thinner, prettier, happier." We're harder on ourselves than anyone else could ever be.

The roots of this unrest are found in the emotional imprints of your childhood. You cannot rewrite history, but you can change how much power you give your inner demons and fears to keep you from being at peace with yourself and leading the life you love.

The choice is yours.

The rewards are immeasurable if, on your path to finding inner peace, you truthfully explore your past with a forgiving heart and open mind and wrap up your worries and "if onlys" in a box addressed to you alone. You can then place this imaginary box on a shelf in the far corners of your mind, where it won't interfere with who you are today and what you will become tomorrow. In this way, peace becomes the greatest gift you can give yourself.

The time to celebrate and put the past behind you is now. The first step toward inner peace is to let go of the you of yesterday…and like it.

Childhood

"There are only two lasting bequests we
can hope to give our children. One of these
is roots; the other, wings."

—Hodding Carter

Anything can be changed.

It is up to you to redirect any negative and painful memories of childhood to a purposeful place in your life. Most of us harbor some painful memories from childhood, how we were treated by our friends, family, parents, siblings, and teachers. Acts that may have happened five, ten, and twenty years ago or more are cast in stone. Yet, emotional scars remain living on in our hearts. The only comfort is that you are not alone.

If you are one of the few who had an ideal childhood and think you could never be a better parent than your parents were, you deserve to be honored as probably one of the luckiest people on the planet. Most of us, while we love our parents and family, can create a rather lengthy list of what we would do differently if we had the chance.

Now is the time to rid yourself of what didn't go right and what you didn't have while growing up. Take a moment to write down all the wonderful experiences of your youth and all that you are thankful for, understanding all the while that all things happen for a reason, that every experience—good *and* bad—served as a stepping stone to today. Next to that list, write down the things that hurt you, that caused you to feel pain, fear, and distrust. On the same piece of paper, next to each of the painful things listed, write a note of forgiveness, of understanding, and of life lessons learned, of how that pain has made you a bigger, better, and stronger human being. Seek to redirect the pain toward a positive, soothing thought of acceptance, understanding, and insight.

You may prefer to reframe your thoughts using your imagination along with, or instead of, the written word. In that case, think of a pleasant thought from childhood—the times when you felt loved, safe, happy, and free. Close your eyes and imagine the colors, brightness, and size of this happy image. Now, think of the painful memory. Take it and make it smaller and duller than the happy memory. As the unhappy memory fades, put it in a tiny corner of your mind where you can't see it. It doesn't deserve a big, bright spot in your life. The positive emotion takes center stage in all its glory and joy.

Know in your heart that your childhood experiences helped to shape who you are today. While much of what occurred was thrust upon you, you have the choice to make the best of it by understanding that hurt and pain go hand in hand with forgiveness and love. You can't have one without the other. The only way to transform the hurt and pain into love is through forgiveness. Forgive those who hurt you and those you hurt. Fully, completely, unconditionally forgive. Forgive with all your heart. If those you want to forgive are no longer here, talk to the heavens above. The message shall be received.

Take your time.

You cannot forgive when you are angry. It's OK to be angry. It's not OK to carry anger around to the point that it interferes with your happiness and peace of mind. Anger keeps you stuck in the past. Your life can't move forward, never mind live fully in the present when anger gets the better of you.

Learning to love the fact that a great part of who you are today is a product of what you experienced yesterday, as a child, opens the door to allow peace to enter and quietly creep into your heart. Let peace in by striving to understand, accept, and, most importantly, forgive any painful memories of childhood. Letting go of the past makes way for the present.

Reflecting on My Finding Peace

Private Point to Consider: Anything can be changed.

Question to Myself: How can I see childhood hurts as necessary life lessons that served to bring me to where I am today?

Acts of Childhood

- Color.
- Paint a picture.
- Bounce a ball.
- Go to a park and play.
- Go to the circus.
- Ride a merry-go-round.
- Jump rope.
- Skip.
- Take an afternoon nap.
- Look through your school picture albums and smile.
- Think about your first best friend.
- Remember the good times and what a giggle feels like.
- Eat a popsicle.
- Blow bubbles.
- Go for a bike ride.
- Roller skate.
- Swing so high you touch the sky.
- Go to a toy store and play.
- Make a sandcastle.

My Acts of Childhood

_____

_____

_____

_____

_____

_____

_____

_____

_____

_____

Parents

"To bring up a child in the way he should go,
travel that way yourself once in a while."
—Henry Wheeler Shaw

You can be the parent you never had.

If you're like most people, no one in the world has more influence on you than your parents. Whether you like it or not, whether you are a parent yourself or not, the truth is that there is no perfection when it comes to parenting. All that can be expected of you, and of your parents before you, is that you do your best with what you've got.

Some parents are blessed with wisdom or financial abundance. Others know the meaning of patience. Still others know how to shower their children with love, hugs, and kisses. Family backgrounds differ, as do each parent's education, priorities, morals, and values. In the end, you are brought into the world as a unique individual with special God-given gifts. The only requirement is that you use your unique gifts and try to do your best with what you've got to be the best parent you can be at the time. And that is all you can expect of your parents.

As a child, you looked to your parents for love, approval, direction, affection, security, and support. Whether your family was rich or poor, small or large, functional or dysfunctional, your parents tried to raise you in the best way they knew how at the time. As an adult, you have the opportunity to question some of the beliefs imparted to you and contemplate the lasting effects of some of the things done to you. Yet, to be able to come to terms with any unresolved feelings and embrace your past with love and forgiveness, you must put these feelings and memories in perspective.

You know the past is over and done. You can't change it. What you can change is how you let it knowingly influence your life. The only way to put the past in its proper place is to forgive. Plain and simple. Forgiveness heals. It is the cure-all for the heart and the only way to fully and lovingly live in the present. Start today by forgiving your mother and father on earth or in Heaven. Talk to them. Talk to yourself. Write a note. Send a letter. Whatever the form, forgiveness is the key.

There are no universities that offer degrees in parenting. You learn it as you go. Your school is the school of life. Your teacher is experience. When you make mistakes, you either learn from them or repeat them over and over. No one can tell you how to do it. Or I should say, others can *tell* you, but you have to learn on your own and make your own mistakes. It was the same for your parents.

The surest way to let go of the past is to be the parent you never had. If your parents never came to your school plays or class parties, go to your children's events. But go with gratefulness and thanksgiving that you have the forgiveness and fullness of heart to give to your children what was not given to you. And go with the understanding that while your parents may not have done this, they may have done the best they could at the time. Maybe they had to work, had marital problems, or had an illness you didn't know about. Understand that they didn't miss your play because of you; that they loved you, but they had something in their lives that kept them from being the kind of parents you wanted them to be. Perhaps it even kept them from being the kind of parents they wished they could be.

When your heart is filled with love, you love. When your heart is filled with pain, you hurt. Be the parent you wish you had and do it with love—love for your parents and love for your children. For as you know, when you treat your children with love, kindness, and understanding, allowing them to explore and nourish their curiosity, to make mistakes, to forgive and to be forgiven, you provide them with the greatest gift of all—room to grow and wings to soar.

Coming to terms with your parents is essential to coming to terms with yourself, with your inner voice that instills the confidence and peace of mind to wake up each day and face the world with joy and purpose. You are probably more critical of yourself than your parents ever were. Maybe your parents said hurtful things now and then, but you probably do it to yourself every day with overly critical thoughts of how you don't measure up. Ask yourself, "How often do I feel stupid, bad, a failure, not good enough, and that my life will never be what I want?" If your answer is every now and then, it's too often.

Let go of being so hard on yourself. Let go of the bad parental voice within and let in the loving and nurturing side of you, the one that comforts and lets you know that things will be OK. Be thankful for what you've got. There are too many forces against us in life.

Sad but true.

You don't need to fight yourself at the same time. You need to love yourself first and foremost. Love is the key.

Reflecting on My Finding Peace

Private Point to Consider: You can be the parent you never had.

Question to Myself: What can I do to understand that my parents did the best they could at the time and that through forgiving them, I can become the parent that I always wished I had?

Acts of Parenthood

- Tell your parents you love them.
- Say "I love you" to your kids at least once a day.
- Ask yourself, "Will this really matter ten years from now?" when you get upset at your children.
- Look forward, not backwards.
- Begin your painful childhood memory with "I forgive you for…" to reframe the event in a light of understanding and love.
- Be the best parent you can be.
- Be the parent you never had.
- Treat your kids with kindness and respect.
- Forgive yourself for any anger and guilt you may feel.
- Remember, you have only one mother and one father.
- Make every day Mother's Day and Father's Day.

- Tell your parents that you are proud of them.
- Tell your parents that you remember what they did to help you get to where you are today.
- Ask your parents what they would have done differently if they could.
- Remind yourself that a parent is simply an imperfect man or woman—and so are you.
- Never stop giving love.

My Acts of Parenthood

_____

_____

_____

_____

_____

_____

_____

_____

_____

_____

Mistakes

"If you have made mistakes…there is
always another chance for you…you may
have a fresh start any moment you choose,
for this thing we call 'failure' is not the
falling down, but the staying down."

—Mary Pickford

I admit I made a mistake.

And so what?

We all have done something wrong, disappointed or hurt people, and said or done things we later regretted. From the time you were a baby trying to walk, falling down, skinning your knees, and banging your head more times than anyone could count, you have been making mistakes. The Bible says that man is not perfect. Knowing in your heart that being human is being imperfect and that you cannot expect more of yourself than you are capable of, you can begin to let go of the fear of failure and open your mind to wanting to take chances and make mistakes in order to grow. The challenge is in not looking at the times you fell, but in sharpening your focus on how many times you've gotten back up. Every mistake you make is an opportunity to learn and grow as a person.

Fear not failing.

Fear not taking chances.

Fear not learning.

Here's a little exercise. Think of the three biggest mistakes you've made in the past—the words you most wish you could take back, the deeds you are ashamed of, and the most pain you may have caused another, intentionally or not. Now, relive the feelings at the time—the hurt, frustration, and embarrassment. Now, take this psychic pain and let it go. Hold it in your hand and blow it up into the heavens. Forgive. Forgive yourself. Ask for forgiveness from those you hurt. Recognize that you are not a bad person. You are human. You may have done bad things and caused pain to others, but it is your actions that are bad, not you.

The most important lesson in life is to learn from your mistakes and not repeat them over and over. In learning how to not repeat the errors of your past, you also learn to ask for forgiveness. If you are fortunate enough to still have the people in your life, try asking for their forgiveness today for the mistakes you may have made in the past. Think about how good you would feel if someone did this to you, if you received a call or letter asking for forgiveness from someone who hurt you and caused you pain.

Being able to admit a mistake builds bridges. After that, the challenge is to not repeat the same ones over and over and learn from the mistakes you make today. Remember my Uncle David's "Words to Remember" in the introduction section of this book? The six most important words are "I admit I made a mistake."

Reflecting on My Finding Peace

Private Point to Consider: I admit I made a mistake.

Question to Myself: How can the mistakes from my past be reframed as life lessons that I see as important turning points and learning experiences?

Acts of Mistakes

- Call a friend to say you're sorry.
- Write a letter asking for forgiveness from those who suffered from your past mistakes.
- Forgive someone today.
- Figure out the things you've learned from the biggest mistakes you've made.
- Make "I'm sorry" a part of your everyday life.
- Try saying to yourself, "So what if I made a mistake? If no one was hurt by it, then what's the worst that can happen?"
- Find the good in imperfection, not perfection.
- Give yourself a break.
- Give others a break.
- Keep trying to get it right—don't give up.
- Think about what you would label a "mistake" today vs. five or ten years ago.
- Think about how you've grown.
- Read the Bible again.
- Know that God forgives.

My Acts of Mistakes

_____

_____

_____

_____

_____

_____

_____

_____

_____

_____

Forgiveness

"Never does the human soul appear so
strong as when it foregoes revenge,
and dares forgive an injury."

—E.H. Chapin

To forgive is divine.

Finding peace of mind begins with forgiving yourself and the people in your past. Forgiveness means letting go of the hurt, pain, anger, and fear that clutter your mind and harden your heart. These unhelpful negative emotions keep you from being the best you can be. They create doubts, not dreams. They break, not build.

When you are unable to find forgiveness, a dark cloud hovers over your life. The sun's healing rays can only shine through once the clouds part. Only love and the forgiveness you find as a result of opening your heart will part the clouds and lift the burden of the past. No wind or outside force will magically erase the pain of the past. Only faith, love, and forgiveness will dull the pain of any unpleasant memories still harbored today.

To forgive unconditionally is to forgive all— yourself, parents, family, friends, old loves, bosses, coworkers, and others you have met along the way. Ask to be forgiven and, at the same time, forgive those who have hurt you. Forgiveness unburdens your heart. A heavy heart knows no peace. Lighten your load and lift your spirits by not only asking for forgiveness, but also, and equally importantly, forgiving others for the hurt they may have caused you.

Forgiveness asks you to be big, to rise above the smallness of holding grudges and harboring animosity, to be bigger than the hard-hearted ways of others, to be, in a sense, godly.

Say a prayer and forgive yourself first.

Reflecting on My Finding Peace

Private Point to Consider: To forgive is divine.

Question to Myself: How can I soften my heart and let forgiveness replace the pain, hurt, and anger toward those who have caused me pain and to forgive myself for the trespasses I have made?

51

Acts of Forgiveness

- Pray for forgiveness.
- Forgive yourself for not being perfect, for hurting others, and for doing things you may not be proud of.
- Focus on the hurtful act when you ask for forgiveness.
- Forgive those you hurt.
- Forgive those who hurt you—even if they don't ask for forgiveness.
- Write a letter to everyone you have hurt, asking for forgiveness.
- Be friends again.
- Look the other way.
- Let unimportant things slide.
- Talk it out.
- Start over again.
- Pick up where you left off.
- Ask those you hurt, "What can I do to make it up to you?"
- Think about what you did that caused hurt and what you have to do to not do that again.

- Reflect on why you did what you did or why the other person did what they did to create a circumstance where forgiveness is needed—what is the real problem?
- Remind yourself that past pains can only hold onto you until forgiveness sets you free.

My Acts of Forgiveness

Acceptance

"Accept the pain, cherish the joys,
resolve the regrets; then can come the
best of benedictions—'If I had my life
to live over, I'd do it all the same.'"

—Joan McIntosh

To those who say, "If only….," you say, "So what. So what if…?"

The past lives on in many people's lives. Why this is so is a mystery to those who want to let go and not hold on. Yet, many find it hard to accept the harsh realities of what they have done and what may have been done to them. Usually, painful memories are the hardest to accept. It is easier to deny that painful events ever happened or to try to change the fact that they did. It seems that the past is capable of taking a gripping hold of our lives.

All the worry and regret in the world can't take back what was said and done long ago. Why waste valuable emotional and mental energy on something you can't change? You do it because you want to regain a sense of control—over your emotions, over others, and over righting your wrongs. Yet, in this case, the way to control the past is to let it go, accept it for what it was, understand what happened, and learn and grow from it. A calmness and clarity arise when you learn to accept what is, rather than think in terms of what should have been. Too often, we look back on our past and think, "If only I had done this," or, "What if that had never happened?"

Now is the time to turn all these "ifs" into "So what ifs?" That's right. So what if I hadn't married so young? So what if I had taken that job? So what if I hadn't said that in the heat of the moment? So what? Thinking about your past in terms of "So what if?" allows you to cast your cares away with the wind. It doesn't change the past—what happened, happened. It doesn't change the pain—what hurts, hurts. What does change is your perspective of the past and its effect on your life today. Your mind can be clear to capture the moment when you accept the past in terms of "So what if?"

The road to peace of mind is fraught with land mines from the past, ready to deter you from living fully in the moment. Maybe it's doubt based on a past failure that creeps in, or fear that overcomes you because you were hurt in a similar situation before. Whatever the nature of the emotional explosion locked in a land mine, it isn't good. It doesn't help you be the best you can be. It doesn't motivate, support, or enthuse. It robs you of enjoying life, taking chances, and savoring the moment.

Accepting the past for what it was, no more and no less, is essential to letting it go and moving on to the present. Acceptance brings you one step closer to finding peace of mind.

Reflecting on My Finding Peace

Private Point to Consider: "So what if…."

Question to Myself: How can I more fully accept my life—with all its pluses and minuses—and my past by changing the "If onlys…." to "So what if…."

Acts of Acceptance

- Love your body.
- Love your mind.
- Love your life.
- Love others.
- Love yourself.
- See your scars as marks of strength.
- Think of the hardest things for you to accept in the past and ask yourself if you would act in the same way today.
- See things for what they were—no more, no less.
- Describe what happened to you or what you may have done in nonjudgmental words and terms, and then objectively assess whether what happened was as painful as you remember.
- Express gratitude for what was because it helped to form the character and person you are today.

My Acts of Acceptance

_____

_____

_____

_____

_____

_____

_____

_____

_____

_____

_____

Purpose

"I began to have an idea of my life, not as the slow shaping of achievement to fit my preconceived purposes, but as the gradual discovery and growth of a purpose which I did not know."

—Joanna Field

There is a reason for all that happens.

Yesterday's events and experiences form the threads of your private life tapestry. The wonderful lines on your face mark the times that have passed in which you experienced joy, laughter, tears, and sorrow. Whether these events scarred your soul or warmed your heart, they happened for a reason and they helped to mold the person you are today.

The challenge is to find the reason not only for why things happened, but for why you are here in the first place. What is the meaning of your life? Only you know the answer to this private and profound question. From deep within, you can begin the search to understand all that has happened, all that is, and all that will be. For there is a purpose to this maddening and wonderful life—each and every one of us has one.

Making sense of the past in terms of the purpose of events that have happened brings comfort.

Think about matters of the heart. Having kissed some toads, you are then able to recognize your prince when he comes along. Having job-hopped for years, you realize more and more what you want, and sometimes, more importantly, what you don't want. Having been stricken with severe illness, you learn how to truly appreciate good health. Having lost someone you love, you learn to not let one day go by that you don't tell the ones you love how much they mean to you.

There is a method to the madness in the grand scheme of life. Some call it divine order. Others call it fate. However you choose to view it, know deep within your heart that there is purpose to your life and all that has gone before you has brought you to where you are today. Particularly, your most painful experiences form your character, though at the time you'd never think so.

By blessing the past, you allow yourself to fully live in the present.

Reflecting on My Finding Peace

Private Point to Consider: There is a reason for all that happens.

Question to Myself: How can I fully explore my life's purpose and understand how who I am today, my talents and energy, has been shaped in part by my past experiences?

Acts of Purpose

- List the building blocks of painful experiences that made you who you are today and have contributed to your character and strength.
- Make a two-column list: the doors that closed on you and the windows that opened.
- Answer the question, "What do I want to be when I grow up?" Then, do it—no matter your age or circumstance, follow your dreams. You'll never regret listening to your heart. You'll only wonder what could have been when you don't.

My Acts of Purpose

_____

_____

_____

_____

_____

_____

_____

_____

_____

_____

_____

Understanding

"We may have all come on different ships,
but we're in the same boat now!"
—Martin Luther King Jr.

Seek to understand, not be understood.

Part of letting go of the past is reaching a level of understanding with the people, places, and events of yesterday. With compassion for yourself and for those who have touched your life, seek to understand, not to simply be understood. Understand why others do what they do. Ask yourself these questions about the actions of others:

- What motivates them?
- What do they want from me?
- What do they fear?
- What do they feel?
- What are they thinking?
- How can I help them?
- Why do they do what they do?
- Am I more perfect?

Through this process of understanding, you bring others closer by building bridges, not divides, and by understanding, not judging. Through seeking to make sense of your past with love and acceptance, you can then more easily come to terms with today. There are no more powerful words than when a friend says "I understand how you feel" and truly means it. Seek to understand and not worry as much about being understood. Seek to accept and not worry as much about being accepted.

Take the first step by understanding you.

Reflecting on My Finding Peace

Private Point to Consider: Seek to understand, not to be understood.

Question to Myself: What can I do to turn the mirror away from my face and listen with an open mind and loving heart?

Acts of Understanding

Ask yourself:
- "Why do I do the things I do?"
- "Would I still do today what I did yesterday?"
- "What drives me?"
- "Why do I associate with certain people?"
- "Why did the ones who hurt me most do the things they did?"
- "Why did I hurt myself and do I still do it?"

Then, give yourself some credit for at least trying to understand why things happen as they do.

My Acts of Understanding

_____

_____

_____

_____

_____

_____

_____

_____

_____

_____

Pride

"Love yourself first and everything else falls into line. You really have to love yourself to get anything done in this world."

—Lucille Ball

To know in your heart that you are unique and beautiful is heavenly. To think any less is merely mortal.

Your past created who you are today—your genetics, culture, religion, ethnicity. The fabric of your being was woven from birth. Take pride in who you are and where you came from. Black. Brown. White. Yellow. Short. Tall. Fat. Thin. Christian. Jewish. Muslim. Buddhist. Mexican. American. African. Chinese. Japanese. European. Woman. Man. Stand straight. Head high. Eyes on the stars. You are unique—a beautiful mix of history, language, color, and spirit. Taking pride in who you are is important if you are to share your life with the world and make the most of the experiences you have, for you are as weak as the secrets you keep.

Accepting your individuality allows you to look outward and not be so preoccupied with what others think, for you really never know what they may be thinking. It is up to you to redirect your images to positive, healthy, and righteous thoughts.

Reflecting on My Finding Peace

Private Point to Consider: To know in your heart that you are unique and beautiful is heavenly. To think anything less is merely mortal.

Question to Myself: What makes me unique?

Acts of Pride

- Recite ten things of beauty about yourself.
- Learn about your heritage.
- Learn the language of your ancestors.
- Reveal your secrets.
- Celebrate rituals of your religion or culture.
- Take pride in the color of your skin.
- Stand up for your country.
- Create a family tree.
- Write your family story.
- Wear high heels if you're tall and go barefoot if you're short.
- Wear a bikini if you're overweight.
- Wear shorts if you have skinny legs.
- Let your roots show if you're not a real blonde.
- Don't be ashamed of being smart, or not so smart for that matter.

My Acts of Pride

_____

_____

_____

_____

_____

_____

_____

_____

_____

_____

_____

Emotions

"Some people feel with their heads
and think with their hearts."

—G.C. Lichtenberg

It is when you let the negative overshadow the positive that you get into trouble.

When thinking of the past, what emotions come to mind? How much of your past is laden with thoughts of joy, pleasure, laughter, and love? Or are your thoughts of sadness, tears, regrets, and pain? All of these emotions are natural, for your past is a mixture of the positive and the negative, the happy and the sad, the yin and the yang. One is as necessary as the other. Just as there is day and night, the sun and the moon, and man and woman, opposites harmonize to create a greater purpose than one alone can do. So it is the same with pain and pleasure, both essential to your spiritual and emotional growth, both necessary to create a life worth living.

Think about champion athletes who visualize victory—every second of their performances are run through their minds until they're perfect. Now, imagine this mental exercise as one of visualizing defeat—falling, not getting up, not doing their personal best. The same is true of our everyday mental imagery. Negative attracts more negative. Positive attracts more positive and makes it easier to overcome the negative.

Now is the time to let go of negative emotions, heal the old wounds, and get on with the business of today. Like many of us, you may store your pain in the darkest recesses of your mind. Only when a crisis erupts or some serious event occurs do you bring forth your deepest fears—fear that things will repeat themselves and that they will be no different, perhaps even worse. And well they may be, for if you continue to harbor negative, painful emotions from the past, whether consciously or subconsciously, you hold yourself back from joy and, ultimately, peace of mind.

In your search for peace, you must continually strive to deal with the emotions of your past, put them to rest, and set them free. You must free yourself of yesterday's burdens and open your heart to the promise of the present. It is no coincidence that "present" is the same word used for both "today" and "gift."

Think of today as the gift you give yourself.

Reflecting on My Finding Peace

Private Point to Consider: It is when the negative overshadows the positive that you get into trouble.

Question to Myself: What can I do to turn down the noise in my mind to maintain joyful thoughts and a positive outlook?

Acts of Emotions

- Smile when you want to frown.
- Don't let the sun catch you crying.
- Laugh it off.
- Draw a happy face in your mind's eye around the person who has hurt you.
- Tell someone you love them.
- Cry your eyes out and feel sorry for yourself for one whole night—then get over it!
- Sing your favorite song in the shower.
- Close the doors and scream your head off.
- Write an honest letter to those who caused you the most pain—and don't mail it.
- Think of the rainbows that follow the rain.
- Contemplate the strength you gained by experiencing all the pain.

My Acts of Emotions

_____

_____

_____

_____

_____

_____

_____

_____

_____

_____

Obstacles

"When you get into a tight place and everything goes against you, 'til it seems as though you could not hang on a minute longer, never give up then, for that is just the place and time that the tide will turn."

—Harriet Beecher Stowe

Obstacles can become opportunities.

Along the way, everyone has experienced obstacles. Perhaps divorce, illness, family problems, hard economic times, legal woes, or even death have taken their emotional toll. Somehow you've straddled the bumps in the road. Maybe you've stepped aside and shielded yourself from the blows. Or perhaps you are one of those who leads a life of silent desperation, putting on a pretty face for the world, yet quietly retreating to your secret world of despair. Or maybe you are in denial about the burdens you carry, or perhaps you face obstacles head on and fight fire with fire. Whatever your particular brand of coping, now is the time to appreciate what you have overcome, the obstacles surmounted, and the strength amassed to rise above life's inevitable challenges.

To some extent, obstacles are what you make of them. One person may see a mean-spirited coworker as an impediment and another may see the same person as a motivating force to do better and shine brighter. Some may see illness as insurmountable while others take it in stride. Still others may see death as a terrible loss while others view it as personally sad, but also as a blessed moment where one's soul can live for eternity in Heaven. Obstacles, in other words, are as big and bright or as small and dull as you make them. They are subject to your interpretation, but you always know one when you have overcome one. You need to pat yourself on the back, as corny as it may sound, when you successfully rise to the challenges that face you. Only you truly know what you've been through. Fear doesn't taste good. Only you can acknowledge and reward yourself for all that you've become. Confidence isn't easily measured, but it can be found in loving again after having lost, finding another job after being fired, or rebuilding your strength after suffering severe illness. Courage in adversity is the stuff of heroes, perhaps not the ones you hear about in the papers, but the ones who may be living next door.

By recognizing past obstacles and acknowledging your accomplishments in overcoming them, you are best prepared for today's challenges. With a heightened sense of self, obstacles can become opportunities.

Reflecting on My Finding Peace

Private Point to Consider: Obstacles can become opportunities.

Question to Myself: What opportunities have been created through the obstacles I have faced in both my personal and professional life?

Acts of Obstacles

- List the top ten things you have overcome and how you are better for having done so. Now, throw away the paper and yell "Hooray!"
- See a glass as half full.
- Eliminate the word "can't."
- Face your fears.
- Make fear a friend.
- Recognize that some people see mountains while others see hills.

My Acts of Obstacles

_____

_____

_____

_____

_____

_____

_____

_____

_____

_____

_____

Baggage

"Living in the past is a dull and lonely business;
looking back strains the neck muscles, causes
you to bump into people not going your way."
—Edna Ferber

If we all put our emotional baggage in a suitcase, there's no doubt it could fill a jumbo jet. But where would we be headed?

Nowhere and fast.

All the baggage that you carry in your life today inhibits your happiness and well-being. To rid yourself of unhelpful feelings from the past, you first must recognize that you are carrying the baggage and be willing to let it go. If you're anything like me, you have a mile-long list of old memories and hurt that couldn't fit into simply one suitcase. No matter. Stuff it all in there and open the door to the plane in mid-flight and throw the suitcase out. Let it fall into a million pieces as it plummets to earth. Who needs it anymore?

The only baggage you'll carry from now on is pleasant, life-affirming thoughts from the past that soothe and comfort. Any other memory is of no use. Only by ridding yourself of this excess baggage can you lift the burden of the past from the present. In the end, the only baggage you'll carry will be the one that holds your bathing suit—perfect for an island getaway.

Reflecting on My Finding Peace

Private Point to Consider: If we all put our emotional baggage in a suitcase, there's no doubt it could fill a jumbo jet. But where would we be headed?

Question to Myself: How can I take my thoughts about the past and relinquish them to fully live in the present?

Acts of Baggage

Think of the things you fear the most and the things that left emotional scars and inhibited your ability to take chances and follow your dreams. Now, carefully imagine wrapping up each of these thoughts and feelings and putting them in a big box. Take the box and seal it tight. Then think of a dark, hidden place in your house, one where you never go, and place the box in that area. It should be a dark and far corner—one where it can never be found.

My Acts of Baggage

_____

_____

_____

_____

_____

_____

_____

_____

_____

_____

_____

Fear

"Nothing in life is to be feared.
It is only to be understood."

—Marie Curie

Fear protects you from danger but also prevents you from living.

You must listen when the little voice tells you that you are at risk, that your health and well-being are jeopardized if you walk down a dark alley or go with a stranger you just met. You must dismiss fear when it stops you from taking chances and trying new things that will help you grow and become bigger, better, and stronger.

Facing your fears means coming to terms with your past. Fear of public speaking may be due to the one time in sixth grade that the class laughed because you had spinach in your teeth. Fear of falling in love again may be due to the time you had your heart broken by the one you loved more than life itself. Fear of career success may be due to the fact you were told that you were stupid your whole life and wouldn't amount to anything. The past invades the fiber of your being as your knees tremble, your stomach aches, and your head pounds with the fear that you won't measure up. As with any self-fulfilling prophecy, you think bad thoughts and bad results follow.

In my daughter's Brownie troop, the girls are awarded "try-its" for completing four new activities in a category of their choosing. For example, they are rewarded for making "ants on a log" and tasting it, even if they don't like peanut butter and raisins on a celery stick. The point is that they tried it. Think about that—little six- and seven-year-old girls getting rewarded for trying something. Now, think about yourself—decades apart in age—and try something new yourself—face your fears.

If you fear commitment, tell the one you love how you feel about him. If you fear success, do nothing less than your very best. If you fear falling, go skiing or parasailing. If you don't like water, go for a swim. Imagine all the wonderful people, places, and experiences that await you. Just remember to do what you think you can't do.

Reflecting on My Finding Peace

Private Point to Consider: Fear protects you from danger but also prevent you from living.

Question to Myself: Am I facing my fears my taking chances, doing what I think I cannot do and discovering all that I can be?

Acts of Fear

- Face your fears by asking yourself, "What's the worst that can happen?" Needless to say, you have survived the hurt, pain, or imagined effects of doing something you were uncomfortable with in the past. You got through that. You will get through this, too.
- Reflect on past events realistically. What really happened? Why am I really afraid?
- Do exactly that which you think you cannot do.
- Tell someone you love that you love him if you're afraid of commitment.
- Lead when you feel you can only follow.
- Speak up when you feel tongue-tied.
- Make a lot of mistakes if you need to be perfect.
- Tell it like it is if you feel you need to hide your true feelings.
- Listen to your heart...and follow it.

My Acts of Fear

_____

_____

_____

_____

_____

_____

_____

_____

_____

_____

_____

The You of Today

Seize the moment. Live life to the fullest. Be honest. Follow your heart. Take chances. Fear nothing and no one. To accomplish these feats, you must never look back. Yesterday's hurts can become either today's worries or valuable lessons. In its proper perspective, the past can be your greatest teacher. The real challenge is to keep your mind on what *is*, not what was or even what will be. Today is fleeting and you miss what's in front of you when you turn your head to look behind you. Imagine driving on the freeway with your eyes permanently affixed to the rearview mirror. That's exactly how dangerous it is to live your life letting the past preoccupy you.

To head in the direction of your dreams and find the peace of mind you so dearly desire, your eyes need to be focused on the moment—one day at a time. Finding peace is a day-by-day process. Sometimes you'll take two steps forward and one step back, and old habits will creep in until you have the strength to overcome them once again. You may be left wondering if you'll ever find your path again after all the constant detours.

The secret is to know that peace is within you this very moment. At times, it's hard to see it with all the noise, worry, and stress of everyday life. But you can feel it gently caress you when you do something you thought you never could do, express your love unconditionally, or give something to someone without expectation of return. The feeling of well-being, satisfaction, and serenity that comes from acting with love instead of judgment, and joy instead of fear—this is what it's like to be at peace. Maybe you've only felt it for a fleeting moment, but its warmth and comfort resonates, warming your soul and soothing your mind.

The best way to awaken the peace that resides within and make it a greater part of everyday life is to focus on the moment—live today to its fullest, fearing less and loving more.

The time is now to come to terms with the past, let go, and move on to live fully, consciously, and passionately in the present. Think of the young child who is having the time of her life, building sand castles and curling her toes in the splashing waves on a hot summer day. The joy of the moment is fully savored by the young and the young at heart. The joyful heart is so busy living the moment that it can't imagine the future nor think of the past. The next time you see a child singing at the top of her lungs or running as fast as the breeze, freeze frame the moment in your mind's eye as a living example of fully being at one with the present.

The you of today is the creator of peace of mind. Yesterday is gone. Tomorrow is yet to be.

Peace of mind lives in the present, moment by moment, in the here and now.

Permission

"You will do foolish things,
but do them with enthusiasm."

—Colette

Give yourself permission to breathe.

Imagine how wonderful it feels to take a big, deep gulp of the most refreshing spring air. In life, every day can be like a spring day if you give yourself the chance to breathe freely and deeply by giving yourself permission—permission to not be perfect, to feel how you feel, to say "no," and to simply *be* instead of having to *do* all the time.

Too often, in this rush-about world, you are running from place to place, appointment to appointment, stoplight to stoplight. Some of this pressure is out of necessity—based on the demands of a two-income family, work, and multiple family responsibilities, such as caring for children or elderly parents. Add to this the commitments that you have to taking care of your own personal life responsibilities, and it's no wonder you forget to take time for yourself—to be good to yourself, to relax, to feel comfort and quiet, to listen to music, or to linger over a cup of tea.

Permission to breathe can mean permission to do nothing, to do whatever you want, or not to do what you don't want to do. It's about flexibility and giving yourself a break. You make the rules and the schedule, but are you making room for downtime? Everything that operates needs maintenance work and refurbishment. Your inner self is no exception. You need downtime to regroup and reenergize. Sometimes it's simply time that is needed. In other cases, it may be experiencing certain sensory activities that soothe and refresh. You know what you like, and it's important to give yourself permission to stop doing, going, running, and achieving and start unwinding, reflecting, decompressing, and renewing your inner spirit. You can't do this on the run, for your inner voice can only be heard in stillness.

Give yourself permission to be as you are—no more and no less. Give yourself permission to cry and to be emotional, lethargic, giddy, dumb, late, wrong—or whatever it is you feel at the moment. Some think sleeping is all the rest you need. On the contrary, some of the best rest you will experience is the kind of rest that occurs when your eyes are wide open. A still mind, awake and in repose, allows the heart to be heard.

Listen to your heart. When you listen closely, and hear its gentle whispers, peace is near.

Reflecting on My Finding Peace

Private Point to Consider: Give yourself permission to breathe.

Questions to Myself: How often am I simply "being" instead of "doing"?

Acts of Permission

- Take a long, luxurious bubble bath.
- Keep the answering machine on.
- Sleep in.
- Get a full-body massage.
- Take a walk in the park.
- Leave the bed unmade and the dishes in the sink.
- Throw away your to-do list.
- Stay in bed all day.
- Sit by the fireplace and dream.
- Do something decadent.
- Sing a new song.
- Say whatever is on your mind for a day.
- Take a vacation.
- Cancel plans and stay home.
- Lose your cool and show how you feel.

My Acts of Permission

_____

_____

_____

_____

_____

_____

_____

_____

_____

_____

_____

Attitude

"Be pleasant until ten o'clock in the morning
and the rest of the day will take care of itself."

—Elbert Hubbard

Anticipate the positive.

Looking at the world through rose-colored glasses is a good idea these days. Things are what they are. If you watch the evening news every night, you have reason enough to be depressed. If you read the morning paper, some mornings you don't want to leave your house. There are a lot of negative stimuli bombarding our senses.

However, it is up to you to choose your worldview by adopting a positive, life-affirming attitude or a negative, fearful one.

Which way do you see life?

If an eight-ounce glass has four ounces of juice in it, it has just that: a measurable amount of liquid. Your interpretation of the glass of juice is another matter. You can choose to see the glass as half full or half empty. Both statements are correct, but which word—full or empty—is more positive? If someone has been out of work for months, do you see them as "between jobs" or "unemployed"? Seeing abundance and what is, versus lack and what isn't, colors your view of life. It is empowering to live life with optimism and a sense of control, goodness, fairness, and fullness.

In your private life, when you expect that 80 percent of the time things will be OK, with the usual little ups and downs, 10 percent of the time you'll be on top of the world, and 10 percent of the time you'll feel like you've hit rock bottom, you are better equipped to live today at 100 percent. A positive attitude isn't a perfect one, but one that is uplifting, empowering, and helpful.

Good attitudes build good lives. With a forgiving heart and an open mind, you invite love to enter your life with a positive outlook. Fear vanishes. Doubts fade. Good things happen because you will it to be so. You do not dwell on the bad, evil, and dark sides of life. You live in the light with hope, confidence, and goodwill toward yourself and others.

You will often find that those who have poor attitudes are afraid of something. They are afraid of rejection, failure, embarrassment, judgment, making mistakes, and on and on. Some are even afraid of good things—of love, success, and happiness. Maybe they feel unworthy or have never experienced goodness in the past, so the pattern is continued. Sadly, the bad attitude comes from within.

The good news is that you have the power to change your attitude from fear to love, despair to hope, negative to positive—to embrace life, not push it away. Four things are needed to help cure a bad attitude:

- You must be conscious of the kind of attitude you possess.
- Then, you must have the desire to will away unhelpful attitudes and replace them with empowering thoughts—I can, I will, I can, I will. You've got to want to feel better and be tired of being depressed or negative.

- You need to control what you can and let go of the things you can't do anything about. Maybe you can't change another person, but you sure can change the amount of time you spend with her and the type of interactions you allow.

- Find a support system. It's important to not feel alone, and surely there are people who care about you and understand what you are going through. Maybe it's a friend. Maybe it's a therapist. Maybe it's a group. As the Bible says, "Seek and ye shall find."

New habits are created day by day. At the core of this process is faith—knowing that all will be well and that things work out as they ought to, whether you know it or not at the time. Have faith in God, in yourself, and in your fellow man. Faith sees you through and lights your path during the tough times.

There will always be moments when you will get down on yourself, no matter how much faith you hold in your heart. If once in a blue moon you're depressed or upset to the point at which you're virtually paralyzed by worry and fear, that's part of being human. As sure as day turns into night, life itself is a cycle of unpredictable highs and lows. You can always count on the fact that nothing stays the same.

When you find yourself down in the proverbial dumps, try lifting your spirits by doing something new or something that will make you feel great. Fresh air and exercise are sure ways to brighten a sulky attitude. Take a nice long walk and leave your watch behind. Have coffee with a friend who will let you know that you're not alone. Sit on a park bench with your eyes open to the sights and sounds around—kids playing, dogs barking, joggers jogging, old-timers telling tales, and leaves whistling in the wind. If you need an attitude adjustment and want to stay at home, why not read a great book or magazine with the phone off the hook? Or, take a luxurious nap or give yourself a facial and manicure. Better yet, pamper yourself and get a professional facial, manicure, or massage. Do something good for yourself at least once a day. A bright attitude beckons peace of mind.

It's OK, too, to wallow in the moment occasionally. Every once in a while, give yourself permission to grieve and feel sorry for yourself. Whether you take the time to soak in your sadness or push it away, know that what separates a positive outlook from a negative one is that the positive knows when it's time to take the next step and let go of what you shouldn't be holding onto.

Reflecting on Finding Peace

Private Point to Consider: Anticipate the positive.

Questions to Myself: What repetitive thoughts, phrases, and actions can I adopt to keep hope alive?

Acts of Attitude

- Tell yourself, "It's OK to feel the way I do," and jump for joy or cry your eyes out. Then, tell yourself, "It's time to let go and move on," and don't hold onto unhelpful thoughts that block you from your better self.
- Don't talk about what makes you sad — it only belabors the point. Talk about happy things instead.
- Find a friend who will let you know you're not alone. Everyone needs a support system.
- Practice visualization and see the reality you want in living color.
- Pray and ask God for the help you need.
- Recite affirmations of uplifting thoughts, such as, "I am capable of doing whatever I choose…I am strong, smart, and honest…I am wealthy and have all I ever hoped for."
- Laugh more.
- Control what you can and let the other stuff go.

My Acts of Attitude

_____

_____

_____

_____

_____

_____

_____

_____

_____

_____

_____

Silence

"Fond as we are of our loved ones,
there comes at times during their
absence an unexplained peace."

—Anne Shaw

When was the last time you experienced complete silence?

The noise in your mind and around you can be distracting at best and deafening at worst. Silence is unfamiliar to most of us. In conversations, we feel uncomfortable if we're not talking. At home alone, many of us keep the television on for company. In our cars, we listen to the radio. When we open the door to our offices, we hear the phones ringing and people buzzing about. When we open the windows in our home, we probably hear the sounds of kids playing, cars driving by, and neighbors working around the house. For most of us, the only time there is complete silence is when we rest.

The soul speaks in silence.

Try sitting or lying in a comfortable place for thirty minutes and just do nothing. This isn't easy. If you are to find peace, you must first slow down to let it in. It will be easy to turn off the television, radio, and telephone and close the door. The challenge is to turn off the noise in your mind…to be silent and feel good about it, to let go of your worries and concerns and let in the open space for peaceful thoughts to flourish. These thirty minutes might feel like an eternity. Afterwards, you'll feel rested, cleansed, and clear-eyed in the quiet of your private world.

If you can't resist doing something in your silence, try meditation, yoga, or tai chi. Listen closely in your silent retreat as the gentle embrace of peace of mind warms your heart and soothes your soul without a whisper.

Reflecting on My Finding Peace

Private Point to Remember: When was the last time you hear complete silence?

Question to Myself: How can I create regular quiet time in my busy life?

Acts of Silence

- Keep outside noise to a minimum when you have the time to be alone and use it for thinking and reflection.
- Pray in a quiet corner.
- Meditate.
- Try yoga.
- Enjoy the relaxing sounds of the waves lapping upon the shore, birds singing in the trees, or the wind rustling the leaves.
- Have a conversation with your soul.
- Make it a point to be silent in conversation with others.

My Acts of Silence

_____

_____

_____

_____

_____

_____

_____

_____

_____

_____

_____

Tolerance

"Tolerance is the positive and cordial
effort to understand another's beliefs,
practices, and habits without necessarily
sharing or accepting them."

—Joshua Liebman

Everyone is comfortable with the familiar.

People generally tend to seek out other people and things that are similar to them and their beliefs, practices, and ideas. It is a grand person who accepts and respects that which is different from them. An even grander person seeks to find that which is different.

To tolerate is to say, "You are different from me—no better and no worse—as I am different from you. And that's just fine with me." By allowing others to be themselves without criticism or judgment, you let go of the need to control them by making them live by the same rules you do. By allowing others to do whatever they want, as long as it is not harmful to others, and to believe in what they want to believe in, you encourage diversity and individual expression. Only then do you practice tolerance.

Tolerance invites peace to gently enter your life with its open heart and loving embrace of all that is unique and different. You clear your mind of negative, limiting thoughts and differences and allow acceptance and friendship to flourish. This is not to say that you should change your belief systems or adopt someone else's behavior. Nor should you ever ask this of another. Rather, tolerating others enables you to give others the space and permission to be who they are. It is the most soulful example of demonstrating respect for your fellow man.

Allowing tolerance to enter your life is liberating. You stop judging and start loving. Your fears and thoughts of differences transform themselves into gestures of acceptance and recognition of all the diversity that makes life so colorful and vibrant. You share the mindset that differences are good and healthy while at the same time realizing that you don't have to share someone's beliefs to respect them. Rather, you tolerate what is unique and different. To tolerate is to welcome inner peace into your life because you strive to neither judge nor condemn, but to respect and understand.

Practice tolerance by role playing and becoming the one you judge. If you have rigid religious beliefs, go to a place of worship different than yours. Learn about the religion. Find the humanity in it. If you have racial preconceptions, spend some time in a neighborhood of the people you judge so harshly. Volunteer some time. Be a big sister. Reach out and build a bridge of understanding. If you want to do this exercise with others, assemble a group and split them up based on certain criteria, such as the color of their eyes. Let only the brown-eyed people do something or have a privilege for the day that the blue-eyed people are denied. Then discuss how it feels to be treated differently simply based on the color of your eyes.

Reflecting on My Finding Peace

Private Point to Consider: Everyone is comfortable with the familiar.

Questions to Myself: How can I demonstrate respect and consideration for those with different beliefs and lifestyles than my own?

Acts of Tolerance

- Reach out to someone in need.
- Give your time to charity.
- Give your money to a cause.
- Bite your tongue.
- Walk a mile in your sister's shoes.
- Count to ten.
- Listen—don't speak.
- Inquire—don't tell.
- Accept—don't judge.
- Live and let live.
- List all the unique things that make the people in your life different and wonderful.
- Relax your most rigid beliefs and reach out to those you hold in contempt.
- Repeat this Biblical passage: "Judge not, lest ye be judged."

My Acts of Tolerance

_____

_____

_____

_____

_____

_____

_____

_____

_____

_____

_____

The Present

"With the past, I have nothing to do;
nor with the future. I live now."

—Ralph Waldo Emerson

Why trade this moment in time for any other?

All you have is today. The past is gone. The future is yet to be. While your body lives in the present, your mind is often stuck in reruns of yesterday's news while you worry about the future. Peace of mind only exists in the present. It has no past and knows no future. Worry about the past and fear of the future are two emotions that keep you from living the moment and rob you of the beauty of today.

Most of us worry about similar things. Let's take one example—finances. What good does it do to worry about your bills? Worrying doesn't get them paid or reduce the potential for more bills to come. Wondering why they got so high is fruitless if you don't change your spending and saving habits today. By focusing on the present, you redirect your thinking toward earning the income to pay off the debt, figuring out a payment schedule that works, not buying the unnecessary item on the credit card today, and maybe even paying cash only for anything outside of the normal household bills. You can make a difference in the present.

Living in the present is living life to the fullest, as if each day were your last. As dramatic as it may sound, you open yourself to simple pleasures and moments in time that escape those whose minds are preoccupied with things other than the here and now. Why think of love lost when you can feel love today? Why think of fear of failure when you can experience the joy of success this very moment? Why worry what the future might hold when you have the gift of life today? Why trade this moment in time for any other?

The simple pleasures of the moment are yours for the asking. All you have to do is take the time to pause by the flowers and savor their scent, hug your children and tell them you love them every chance you get, appreciate the colors of the landscape around you, savor the smells of the food you are cooking, and give thanks to the Lord for the gift of life and waking up to a brand new day. Living today to its fullest without cluttering your mind with past hurt and future fears is pure, unadulterated freedom to enjoy not what was, nor what could or should be, but what is—in all its divine glory.

Reflecting on My Finding Peace

Private Point to Consider: Why trade this moment in time for any other?

Questions to Myself: How can I make the present—today—a gift I give myself?

Acts of the Present

- Stop and smell the roses whenever you can.
- Appreciate ten things of beauty.
- Call or write those you'd like to thank—pick someone new every day.
- Catch yourself worrying and adjust the intensity.
- Don't look back.
- Live fully in the moment with an open heart.
- Live as though this were the last day of your life.
- Think about what you have (not necessarily in material terms) and don't focus on what you don't have.
- Take the time to appreciate all you are—savor the thoughts and remind yourself of them often.
- Say "I love you" every day to those you love.
- Be thankful for each new day for with it comes a new start.

My Acts of the Present

_____

_____

_____

_____

_____

_____

_____

_____

_____

_____

Happiness

"The greatest happiness you can
have is knowing that you do not
necessarily require happiness."
— William Saroyan

Happiness is found in who you are, not what you do or how much you have. Happiness is a state of mind. Think happy thoughts, be happy. Think unhappy thoughts, be unhappy.

You can find happiness today if you only look. It's right next to you. Look into the eyes of your child. Reach out to hold your husband's hand. Give a friend the hug she needs. Happiness is found in the here and now, in the people who touch your life and whose lives you touch. Happiness is found in the body, life, and spirit you live with today in all its imperfections and uniqueness. Happiness can't be seen with the naked eye. During trying times, happiness comes in the form of blessings in disguise—invisible to the naked eye.

No amount of money, possessions, or ego gratification can bring you happiness. There is no such thing as the perfect car, house, job, or person to make you happy. Peace of mind comes with the recognition that happiness is totally and unequivocally in your control. Like turning on a light to illuminate a darkened room, feelings of joy and bliss are yours when you choose to turn on your inner light, which is forever charged and ready to shine.

Your attitudes and beliefs can keep you from the light. Sometimes you can get caught up in the drama of the moment and allow doubt and fear to set in. Doubt and fear can be beneficial when these emotions serve to better prepare you for real land mines you are about to face. They can keep you out of harm's way. More often, doubt and fear override your resolve and keep you from realizing your dreams.

The key is to push the unhelpful emotions aside and replace them with empowering thoughts of lessons to be learned and strength to be gained from facing your fears. Much like a new pair of glasses improves your vision, a new attitude can provide a clearer, brighter outlook. Let in light and clarity and allow your soul to soar. Visualize the possibilities! As unproductive, unhelpful thoughts creep into your consciousness, replace them with brighter and larger images that empower and uplift.

It is also important to contemplate your particular definition of happiness. Ask yourself, "Is it realistic to expect what I expect of others and, more importantly, of myself?" Listen to your answer.

You will always be disappointed if your expectations are unrealistic. It's all in how you view it. In personal relationships, one person will find another to be a wonderful mate—loving, handsome, compassionate, and kind—while another would be disappointed in the same person, viewing him as unattractive and selfish.

One is happy with a hug. The other wants roses and candlelight dinners. One looks at her mate's beauty from within. The other obsesses on her mate's love handles and double chin. In the end, you see what you want to see and feel what you want to feel. The secret to finding lasting happiness is seeing the invisible, that which can't be seen by the naked eye, that which lives in your very soul. During good times, it's easy to be happy. During trying times, seek that which is unseen—blessings in disguise.

Reflecting on My Finding Peace

Private Point to Consider: Happiness is found in who you are, not what you do or how much you have.

Question to Myself: How can I make it easier on myself to think happy thoughts?

Acts of Happiness

- Make a list of what you've always wanted, then fill in the blanks with all that you have in your life today, focusing on things of the soul.
- Think back to when you were happiest. What was going on in your life then? What do you need to do to invite happiness in today?
- Define happiness—keep it realistic and attainable.
- Reassess your expectations of life. Know that you can still be a happy person through the roughest of times.
- Give of yourself to others.
- Do something for yourself every day.
- Make a friend.
- Be a friend.
- Smile in sadness.
- Renew your faith in God and know that you are blessed.
- Count your blessings.
- Find the blessings in disguise.

My Acts of Happiness

_____

_____

_____

_____

_____

_____

_____

_____

_____

_____

_____

Pain

"It is the fire of suffering that brings
forth the gold of godliness."
—Madame Guyon

Pain knows no boundaries.

The experience of loss may be universal, but how we deal with loss creates character. We have all been hurt. One we loved has disappointed us along the way. Old lovers, friends, and family have let us down at some point. Perhaps it was when we needed them most, or when we weren't looking. We have all also been slighted at one time or another in our jobs. All too familiar is the memory of a bruised ego as a result of not getting a promotion or deflated spirits when we weren't recognized for our hard work.

Though it may not feel like it while in the throes of gut-wrenching pain, you grow and gain strength as you work through the loss, the hurt, and the confusion. Perhaps you learn to appreciate what you have after losing someone close to your heart. Maybe you feel strengthened by simply surviving the experience and not giving up. Maybe you discovered powers you never thought you had because you were able to actually help a close friend through her loss. Pain teaches you in unexpected ways how to be wiser and stronger, how to face your fears and not run away from them, and how to strengthen your resolve to rise above loss and find the blessings in disguise.

It hurts to fall down and skin your knee. As a child, if you hadn't fallen so often, you wouldn't know the joy of riding a bike or even walking. Feeling pain is essential to feeling alive. The question isn't how to negate it; rather, it's how to face it head on and deal with it so you come out better on the other end.

Like many others, you may have a tendency to not allow a wound to heal. With emotional wounds, it takes time and forgiveness to let go of pain. Wallowing in loss, holding grudges, harboring anger and resentment, and being judgmental of others will do no good. The pain, though it may be buried or hidden from view, lingers and chips away at your very soul.

To find peace of mind, you must come to terms with pain and its value and role in your life. Expect pain to occur in everyday life. Strive to learn from it. Recognize why you feel hurt. It's OK to work your way through the loss and mourn. Then, give yourself time. Time heals. With pain in your heart, there is no room for peace to enter. Welcome peace by welcoming pain as a necessary teacher in life. Welcome peace by forgiving and moving on.

Reflecting on My Finding Peace

Private Point to Consider: Pain knows no boundaries.

Question to Myself: How can I accept the pain in my life and learn to work through my emotions to come out stronger and be a better person for having done so?

Acts of Pain

- Forgive....Forgive...Forgive.
- Look at what you have left, not what you've lost. Are you wiser for having gone through the pain? Are you blessed from having experienced love, even if it didn't last? Are you stronger now that you know what to do in the face of adversity?
- Be thankful for feeling when so many are numb to life. Feel pain as you feel pleasure—as proof that you are alive.
- List what you've learned from the most painful moments in your life—how are you better, stronger, and wiser as a person for having gone through the loss and rough times?
- Ask for forgiveness when you have caused pain.
- Take your time, for time heals all.

My Acts of Pain

_____

_____

_____

_____

_____

_____

_____

_____

_____

_____

_____

Criticism

"Nobody can make you feel
inferior without your consent."

—Eleanor Roosevelt

Now is the time to silence the inner critic.

Criticism is everywhere. People are paid to critique the movies you see, the books you read, and the products you buy. In our own lives, we often tend to be our own worst critic and hurt ourselves in the process. Have you ever exaggerated in your own mind a passing comment your boss may have made and suddenly think you're going to get fired? Do you find that when your friend comments that you look good today, you think to yourself, "That means I must not look good all the time"? Do you think of all the things you do wrong and not all that you do right?

Know that you are doing your best with what you've got, and that's good enough. Once you begin to lighten up on yourself, you can open your mind to others and lift the veil of judgment that only builds walls. It's exhausting to perpetually be self-critical. Give yourself a break and leave the critiquing to the experts.

When it comes to others being personally critical of you, try focusing on the behavior they are talking about. When people communicate in terms of behavior, there is less defensiveness. For example, saying "You're bad" instead of "What you did was bad" personalizes the comment and creates barriers and hurt feelings. Try translating what the critic is saying, even if he doesn't know how to say it best. Focus on the behavior or action he is talking about, not the way he says it, which may seem like a personal attack.

Being the recipient of criticism can be strengthening when you look for the grain of truth in the comment. Sometimes criticism has no value but to hurt, but when there is a grain of truth to be found, look for it. For even in the hard-hearted ways of others, you can find yourself.

Reflecting on My Finding Peace

Private Point to Consider: Now is the time to silence the inner critic.

Question to Myself: Do I remember to ask these three simple questions before I say, do, or think anything that is critical whether to myself or others· Is it kind? Is it necessary? Is it true?

Acts of Criticism

- Be constructive in your comments.
- Focus on behaviors, not personality.
- Be specific, not general.
- Critique with love, not judgment—be a supportive coach.
- See the silver lining.
- Give someone the benefit of the doubt.
- Give yourself the benefit of the doubt.
- Remember the Bible— "Judge not, lest ye be judged."
- Find the grain of truth in critical comments.
- Ask others for their opinions.
- Make criticism constructive—use words that build, not break.

My Acts of Criticism

_____

_____

_____

_____

_____

_____

_____

_____

_____

_____

Serenity

"If you do not find peace in yourself,
you will never find it anywhere else."
— Paula A. Bendry

Serenity is a state of mind.

Imagine sitting on a rock, perched above a still lake at sunrise. In the distance, all you hear is the hushed chirping of the birds as the wind gently whistles through the leaves. No one is around, only you, at one with nature. Now, take this picture, transpose the feeling it generates, and store it in your mind. Keep it close to your heart. Serenity is indeed a state of mind. It is the calm, clear way in which we live, think, and breathe. Serenity takes place in stillness. Quiet the noise in your mind to let serenity take its place in your heart.

In their desire to find serenity, some pray, meditate, chant, or practice other rituals. The goal is to relax the mind, still the noise, and remove the clutter. Everyone is unique, different in lifestyle, tastes, and desires. Find what is comfortable for you, what feels easy and natural. Serenity is effortless. The more you try to find it, the more it eludes you. In your quest to find serenity and peace of mind, try taking some moments out of your busy schedule to be still, reflect, and be at one with nature and all that is the world around you. Give yourself the free space and time to discover how to relax your mind and ease your worries. Experiment with different places and rituals. Find the one that feels good.

Remember that, at its core, serenity is a product of faith. Renew your faith in God and pray. Ask for help. Pray for guidance. Seek to live your life with a sense of balance in which you spend your energy on the important things. In so doing, you keep a steady pace and prevent one aspect of life from controlling the others. The language of serenity is prayer. As the Bible says, "Seek and ye shall find."

Reflecting on My Finding Peace

Private Point to Consider: Serenity is a state of mind.

Question to Myself: How much am I concerned in the moment with "being" rather than "doing" or "having"?

Acts of Serenity

- Do nothing.
- Allow enriching, affirming thoughts into your life.
- Pray.
- Ask God for guidance.
- Have faith that all things happen for a reason.
- Reach out to others to find your own personal peace.
- Slow down.
- Be still.
- Focus on what is in the here and now—not the "coulddas," "shoulddas," and "woulddas."
- Practice forgiveness, of both yourself and others.
- Simplify—do more with less.
- Seek balance—don't let one aspect of life take over at the expense of all the other things you hold dear.

My Acts of Serenity

_____

_____

_____

_____

_____

_____

_____

_____

_____

_____

_____

Satisfaction

"There's nothing half so real in life as the things
you've done…inexorably, unalterably done."
                                        —Sara Teasdale

Do you focus on what you want or what you need?

In your constant need to attain, grow, acquire more, and become all that you can be, you may often find yourself dissatisfied with your life and those around you. On the one hand, it is OK to be dissatisfied when you turn this emotion into productive, constructive action. Being dissatisfied can be a motivator to try harder, do better, and be your best. However, being dissatisfied and simply complaining or bemoaning your fate and doing nothing about changing yourself and your life's circumstances is not OK. Doing nothing is dangerous, and it's an easy trap to fall into.

Seeking satisfaction in all that you are allows you to become all that you can be. Seeking satisfaction takes energy. Being dissatisfied doesn't. If you strive to accept yourself and find pleasure in your life, you walk in life with strength and empowerment. Victims see the world in terms of things being done to them. The strong see the world in terms of the things they can do.

Satisfaction—feeling deeply and fully satisfied with yourself and the life you are building—is achieved in much the same way as a house is built. Each time you feel satisfied with yourself, you add another emotional and psychological building block to the foundation of self-esteem that will bring you shelter and comfort through the bad times and empowerment and support through the good times. But it can only happen one brick at a time.

Satisfaction is built on the smallest of things, the little moments in time that build relationships and create memories. It's when you did what you thought you couldn't or gave what you thought you didn't have. It's when you helped instead of hurt. It's the smile you gave to another. It's the sense of self you created by facing your fears. It's about looking forward, not backwards.

Think about your own personal experiences that could be wonderful examples here.

Work on honestly believing in and regularly reminding yourself of this affirmation: "I am doing my best with what I've got right now."

At this time in your life, affirm over and over again that you are truly doing your best. It's not to say that you can't or won't get better down the road. All it means is simply that today, at this moment in time, you are truly doing your best with your God-given gifts. And that says a lot.

Reflecting on My Finding Peace

Private Point to Consider: Do you focus on what you want or what you need?

Question to Myself: How do I appreciate the little things in life and feel that I am doing the best with what I've got and who I am right now?

Acts of Satisfaction

- Give thanks for all that you are and all that you have.
- Appreciate the little things in life.
- Love the wrinkles and laugh lines that mark the experiences that make you who you are today.
- Love the gifts you've been given.
- Love your body.
- Respect yourself.
- Love others.
- Lend your time and energy to a cause greater than your own.
- Focus on the little things that give great joy.
- Make your self-talk empowering and affirm, "I am doing my best with what I've got right now."
- Reflect on those in your past and remind yourself that they, too, did the best with what they had at the time and forgive, forgive, forgive.

My Acts of Satisfaction

_____

_____

_____

_____

_____

_____

_____

_____

_____

_____

Love

"I never loved another person
the way I loved myself."

—Mae West

Love heals.

Love enters your life through others once you begin to love yourself. At the awesome, inspirational point when you can say, without hesitation, that you know yourself—your strengths and weaknesses, the good and bad—and you love yourself, in spite of it all…this is the point where love can grow. You are its seed.

Self-love waters the soul and forgiveness nourishes the spirit. The values and morals you live by are the foundation for self-acceptance through which love grows. You then can begin to selflessly give and be other-directed.

To give without return. This is the stuff love is made of.

Love and anger don't mix. To bring love into your life, you need to come to terms with any anger you are harboring. Ask forgiveness from those whom you may have hurt, intentionally or not. Forgive yourself for the deeds you aren't proud of and that fanned the flames of anger. Forgive those who have hurt you, intentionally or not. Love enters when anger departs. Forgiveness opens the door.

Love dares not judge. Love accepts.

Love dares not lash out. Love caresses.

Love dares not give with conditions. Love is unconditional.

As you gain wisdom with years, you come to understand that love is not something given to you. Rather, you give love to yourself when you let it in and open your heart to embrace the essence of life. The reason you are here is to love and to be loved in return. Remember to always follow your heart. You'll only regret the times you didn't.

Reflecting on My Finding Peace

Private Point to Consider: Love heals.

Question to Myself: How can I share my love with others—to give without return—and love myself more at the same time?

Acts of Love

- Seek to understand and don't worry about being understood.
- Give without return.
- Say "How can I help?" more often.
- Stand naked in the light of day with your body and soul uncovered…and give yourself a long and loving hug for the wonder of you.
- Forgive yourself for being imperfect.
- Pray for the ones who have hurt you in the past and wish them only good.
- Give of yourself anonymously.
- Remind yourself that God loves you.
- Be a friend to someone in need.
- Make a list of all your wonderful talents and attributes.
- Find ways to complete yourself by exploring your dreams and fears.
- Look at the inside of people you meet— the light that shines from within— instead of outward appearances.
- Follow your heart. You won't go wrong.

My Acts of Love

_____

_____

_____

_____

_____

_____

_____

_____

_____

_____

Friendship

"True friendship is like sound health, the value
of it is seldom known until it is lost."

—Charles Caleb Colton

I love you because I need you or I need you because I love you.

Remember the Barbra Streisand song that goes, "People who need people are the luckiest people in the world"? That song sums up everyone's basic need to be needed. We are not solitary creatures. We want to be part of a group, with people around us who are supportive and nurturing, similar to us in values and interests. Friends satisfy this need.

Your friends are your best support system. It has been said that people who have successfully made it through very stressful times attribute their accomplishment, in large part, to having a good support system. When a caring person listens and lends support and you feel understood, stress levels recede and your sense of well-being is strengthened.

Look at your life today and think about who your true friends are. Let them know you love them. Call on them when you feel down. Cherish them. Make time to make memories with them. They are your safest haven from everyday storms. Be good to your friends and they will be good to you. Know in your heart that you are not alone.

Reflecting on Finding Peace

Private Point to Consider: I need you because I love you or I love you because I need you.

Question to Myself: Who are my true friends and when is the last time that I told them how much I appreciate having them in my life?

Acts of Friendship

- Call a friend to tell her you love her.
- Spend time with an old friend and laugh a lot.
- Make a new friend.
- Renew an old friendship.
- Be a friend to someone in need. Listen and ask, "How can I help?"
- Treat your family as well as you do your best friend.
- Treat yourself as well as you do your best friend.
- Let a friend know that you were just thinking of her.
- Seek not to be understood, but to understand.
- Listen, don't judge.
- Ask for help when you need it.

My Acts of Friendship

_____

_____

_____

_____

_____

_____

_____

_____

_____

_____

_____

Comparisons

"Until you make peace with who you are, you'll
never be content with what you have."

—Doris Mortman

Why not accentuate the positive?

Whether we like to admit it or not, we are constantly comparing ourselves to others, or to an image we have in our mind. Whether we are comparing our possessions ("Their house is nicer." "Their yard is bigger." "I wish I had a car like theirs." "Her diamond is so much bigger than mine.") or our own person ("She's got such a great figure." "Her skin is so flawless." "I wish I was as tall as her." "She has such a flat stomach."), the list goes on and on and on. It doesn't have to. Just look at the person driving next to you or the billboard in front of your face as you inch down the highway at rush hour. It all gets tiring. We can endlessly compare ourselves and come up short every time.

Essential to the process of finding peace of mind is letting go of comparing yourself to any-one. "If only I was this" or "I should be that" are unhelpful one-note sambas that keep you from your dreams. Only by respecting yourself and appreciating your unique God-given gifts can you move forward and be all you can be. The key is to look within, search your soul, and discover the wonder right before your very eyes. For if you don't, you'll find that someone will always have more, better, and bigger things. You'll never measure up when you compare yourself to others.

Instead of envying others, why not accentuate the positive? There is enough abundance in the world for everyone. No one person has a lock on money, beauty, talent, intelligence, love, compassion, or success. Admire and appreciate the wonderful qualities of others, and those same qualities will find their way into your life. Know that you can do whatever you put your mind to and be all that you can be. Know this inside. When you are alone in your room at night, know this. Repeat this affirmation: "I can do whatever I put my mind to. I can be all that I want to be. I believe in me."

Peace of mind can't be bought, sold, or bartered. It comes from within. When you think in terms of yourself, about being the best that you can be by using your own unique God-given gifts, you empower. To do any less is self-destructive. Just as a daisy is no more beautiful than a lily, or a rose is no more perfect a flower than a dahlia, human beings cannot be compared and, in fact, should be appreciated for our unique, distinct, and personal characteristics that make us who we are. There is no other you. So stand tall and let your soul shine through.

Reflecting on My Finding Peace

Private Point to Consider: Why not accentuate the positive?

Question to Myself: How often do I tell myself that I can do whatever I put my mind to— to be all that I can be and that I believe in me?

Acts of Comparisons

- If you're short, admire someone tall.
- If you're short, go barefoot.
- If you're tall, admire someone short.
- If you're tall, wear high heels.
- If you're a blonde, admire a brunette.
- If you're a dyed blonde, let your roots shine through.
- If you're poor in monetary wealth, act like you are rich in spiritual wealth.
- Delight in differences.

My Acts of Comparisons

_____

_____

_____

_____

_____

_____

_____

_____

_____

_____

Doubt

"There are two ways to slide easily through life:
to believe everything or doubt everything;
both ways save us from thinking."

—Alfred Korzybski

Are you ever really sure?

You marry the one you want to be with for the rest of your life. Yet, in secret, you wonder if you are making the right decision. Maybe you are bothered by fleeting thoughts of how he treats you at times. Perhaps the memory of your first love creeps in and you wonder about what could have been. Still, you go forward believing that you are following your heart.

Or, take a more mundane example, like buying a car. At first, it seems perfect. Then, you start to think: *Which color would be the best? Can I really afford it? Is there enough space? What about a smaller car, or a sportier one?* Making choices in life, from the big ones to everyday matters, involves some degree of uncertainty about what is about to follow. How you live with this doubt is what makes the difference in whether you live in neurosis or nirvana. I daresay most of us would choose the latter.

Once you have made a decision, you probably begin to rationalize your choice as the right thing to do. This is completely normal. You want to protect and justify the decision you made because you believe that it reflects upon your character and how others perceive you—as good or bad, smart or stupid, kind or mean. You push aside your gnawing doubts and justify to yourself that you did the right thing. You tell yourself that you're OK—it's the other guy who needs help, who is wrong, who is crazy.

Who, when asked, says they don't like their new car? *It's great. I'd do it all over again.*

Who, when asked, says their newlywed life is anything other than blissful? *There's nothing like it. He's wonderful.*

Who, when confronted by another parent, or even a friend, readily admits to her child's bad behavior or faults? *Don't talk about my child that way. I raise her the best way I know how.*

Who, when asked, really wants to admit that the person she hired is not very good? *Oh, she's still on the learning curve. Give her time.*

Yet, deep within, in the privacy of thoughts that you share with no one, you wonder. You wonder if you've done the right thing, or where another path might have led. Understand that these thoughts are OK to some degree. However, you need to pause when they overtake your better sense of self and prevent you from making the best of your life today. Mindless doubting, the kind that looks back in despair and regret, is hurtful. Mindful doubting, the kind that looks forward to making wiser choices, is helpful.

A peaceful mind may doubt, but it does so with an eye toward tomorrow, in the hopes of making new and better choices, not in mere reflection on things that can't be undone. You invite peace to enter when you recognize the value of doubt and let it have a useful role in your life. Mindless doubt, the kind that is stuck in regrets and sorrow, keeps peace at bay. Letting go of this kind of "what if-ing" makes room for the surety that what happens to you has a purpose.

Know deep inside that your choices have brought you the experiences and lessons that have served to carry you to where you are today. Your choices fulfilled a purpose in creating your world and will continue to do so as you move on the path toward greater peace of mind. When you follow your heart and make decisions with forethought and circumspection, you can't go wrong at that moment in time.

Reflecting on My Finding Peace

Private Point to Consider: Are you ever really sure?

Question to Myself: How can I make doubt work for me to make it useful and purposeful rather than mindless "what if-ing?"

Acts of Doubt

- Repeat, "So what if…?" every time you find yourself doubting your choices.
- Ask yourself, "What's the worst that can happen?"
- Try being a little more honest and less protective when there may be a valid reason for critiquing your decisions.
- When you are reflecting on choices you made in the past, think about the downside to what could have been, not just the rosy version.
- Listen to the essence of the doubt because its core may have value.
- Find the grain of truth in criticism.
- Make a list of the pros and cons for the decisions you've made to remind yourself of why you did what you did at the time.
- Think of how you'd do things differently today to make doubt constructive.
- Take personal responsibility for the choices you've made—don't be a victim.

My Acts of Doubt

_____

_____

_____

_____

_____

_____

_____

_____

_____

_____

Reality

"It is good to have an end to journey toward;
but it is the journey that matters in the end."

—Ursula K. Le Guin

Accepting your life for what it is and not what it was or what it could be is an essential step toward finding inner peace.

Too often, we cloud our vision of the world and our lives with beliefs that don't reflect reality. We think people are mad at us, don't like us, or have intentionally done something bad to hurt us. We don't realize that this reality is of our own making.

The "real" reality, the one that exists independent of anyone's personal spin, is often very different. The person whom you think has intentionally done you wrong may have acted out of fear for his own security—his actions may have had nothing to do with you. More often than not, people are driven by their own private demons. They act out of fear—fear that they will be discovered for who they truly are, that they can't measure up, or that they can't succeed.

Driven by this fear and paranoia, people continue to think that everything that is done somehow relates to them and remain blind to the fact that everyone else is actually motivated by the same self-centered emotions. It's a frustrating cycle that can only be broken by the realization that we are all much more similar than different.

Fortunately, when you make this realization, reality becomes clearer and kinder. You stop looking at others in terms of what they have done to you and start trying to understand what could have motivated them to act as they did and think *How can I help?* You begin to accept the fact that reality isn't always pleasant and perfect. You come to expect the inevitable ups and downs and realize that nothing lasts forever—the good times or the bad. You learn to take one day at a time and savor the moment, for that is all you have in hand.

By looking at reality with 20/20 vision, you will undoubtedly enrich your world. Look at your life today. Count the many blessings that you have. Affirm some of the blessings that may apply to you this very moment:

I have a family that loves me.

I have wonderful children.

I am in good health.

My family is in good health.

I am alive.

I have a job.

I have a job that I love.

I have a home.

I own my own home.

I am independent.

I have friends who care about me.

I am able to give to others.

I am in a loving relationship.

I am married.

I have found God.

Blessings come in many shapes and sizes. Focus on the little things that bring you pleasure and create a sense of personal satisfaction. Understand that all that you have today is borrowed. You came into this world alone and will leave the same way. All the possessions and people you have in your life won't come with you when it's your time to go. These things and relationships are borrowed from God. The legacy you leave in the lives you have touched and the people you have loved makes reality matter.

Look at what you have, not what you lack. Look at what is, not what could be. Remember that others, like you, are driven by internal forces, so don't take everything personally. And, most of all, be kind to yourself. You are your own best friend. Count the many blessings that are you.

Reflecting on My Finding Peace

Private Point to Consider: Accepting your life for what it is and not what it was or what it could be is an essential step toward finding inner peace.

Question to Myself: Am I honest and kind to myself when I look at my life?

Acts of Reality

- Live within your means.
- Count your blessings…then keep counting.
- Pinch yourself.
- Remember what you dreamed of and hoped for as a child and look at all that you have realized in your life.
- Take the mirror from your face in conversations with others. Listen and say only "How can I help?"
- Know that no one's life is perfect, even though it may appear so.
- Accept that reality goes through phases—ups and downs, pleasure and pain, gain and loss, winning and losing.
- Find the blessings in disguise.
- Live the legacy you want to leave. What do you want others to feel about you after you are gone? Live your reality today to fulfill your legacy of tomorrow.

My Acts of Reality

_____

_____

_____

_____

_____

_____

_____

_____

_____

_____

Health

"Vitality! That's the pursuit of life, isn't it?"

—Katharine Hepburn

You have nothing if you don't have your health.

Feeling good, energetic, and alive is an important ingredient in finding inner peace. Good health, apart from the gift of genetics, comes from taking care of yourself, eating right, exercising, sleeping well, enriching your mind, and soothing your spirit. Most of us are so busy and stressed that we grab a bite on the run and exercise on our way to the car and back while we try to get the closest parking spot to the door. We're lucky if we find time to pray, relax, and do nothing. Now is the time to change all that.

Develop a program that will work for you, one that won't cause you more stress and will be a welcome change in your life. Watch your diet—look at ways to eat more fresh fruits and vegetables and do away with sugars, bad fats, and fast-food solutions. Make time to exercise—go to the gym, walk the stairs instead of taking the elevator, jog in place as you watch television instead of simply sitting on the couch, park in the spot farthest from the entrance and walk a little more, buy that exercise tape and get up earlier to do it, or walk during your lunch hour. Exercise your mind—go to the library or bookstore and get a few mind-enriching books that interest you, go to that seminar you've always been curious about, get an audio tape about positive attitudes and any other subject that interests you, or start that hobby you've always been interested in. Enrich your soul—go to church or temple, pray more, read the Bible, talk to God, laugh more, and cry less. Take care of yourself—go get a checkup and try some preventive medicine and homeopathic remedies.

Look at your mind, body, and spirit, for health is three-dimensional. Being in good health is a gift you give yourself. Once you have achieved and can maintain a state of health, you can turn your attention to other things and live your life with vigor and energy.

Your health is something to be cherished. You don't appreciate it until you lose it. If you are in good health, keep it that way. If you are not feeling your best, explore what you need to do with your mind, body, and spirit to feel better. If you are in poor health, do what you can to help yourself. When there is little left to do, pray. Prayer is sometimes your best medicine.

Reflecting on My Finding Peace

Private Point to Consider: You have nothing if you don't have your health.

Question to Myself: How can I take better care of my physical, mental, emotional, and spiritual health?

Acts of Health

- Eat smart.
- Do exercise you find fun.
- Get a massage.
- Walk.
- Drink lots of water.
- Get a checkup.
- Think positive, affirming thoughts.
- Visualize wellness and fighting the illness that may afflict you.
- Get a good night's sleep.
- Sing.
- Dance.
- Laugh.
- Meditate.
- Treat yourself to a spa.
- Go on a diet, and do it for your overall health, not to fit into a smaller dress size.
- Change your lifestyle for the better.
- Pray.
- Seek spiritual support.

My Acts of Health

_____

_____

_____

_____

_____

_____

_____

_____

_____

_____

_____

Spirit

"It isn't until you come to a spiritual
understanding of who you are…that
you can begin to take control."
—Oprah Winfrey

Our time on Earth is borrowed.

God's gift to us is life. When we contemplate that we will leave this world as we have entered it, material possessions and money lose their meaning. We can't take them with us and surely they have no place in Heaven. It is the things of the spirit that really count.

What you are goes beyond the physical, beyond that which you can see. Your spirit is the essence of who you are as a person. It is the light that shines from within that houses your love of life, outlook, attitudes, and sense of well-being. Nourishing this spirit takes commitment and discipline. It's too easy to get down on yourself and those around you. Your ego is constantly trying to inch its way into every waking moment, focusing on all that is not spiritual.

The way to elevate your spirits is through prayer. Getting in touch with God and forming a relationship of your own particular making gives you the strength to make it through the rough times and feel the beauty of being blessed during the good times. Faith is the key and prayer is what gets you there.

In everyday life, you can lift your spirits and those of others with the little things you do. Wear a smile instead of a frown. Laugh more. Sing out loud. Compliment yourself. Pay a compliment to someone else. Say "I love you" to someone every day. Each time you lift a spirit, you become more open to the positive. It's easier to look on the bright side. And, in so doing, your life becomes brighter from the light that shines within.

Peace of mind is yours for the asking. Prayer and positive thinking are the answer.

Reflecting on My Finding Peace

Private Point to Consider: Our time on earth is borrowed.

Question to Myself: How can I nourish my spirit and be all that I can be?

Acts of Spirit

- Smile.
- Laugh.
- Sing.
- Dance.
- Treat people the same when no one is looking as you would in a crowd.
- Pray.
- Find your faith.
- Ask God for help.
- Believe in something bigger than the material world.
- Show compassion by always asking, "How can I help?"
- Build your spirit by being other-directed—giving to others.
- Forgive yourself and ask to be forgiven.
- Give your spirit time to soar—create quiet, reflective time.
- Read inspirational books.
- Keep the faith.

My Acts of Spirit

_____

_____

_____

_____

_____

_____

_____

_____

_____

_____

_____

Mind

"The best mind-altering drug is the truth."

—Lily Tomlin

The power of the mind is breathtaking.

You have the ability to influence your state of health and feelings of happiness through your brain. Your thoughts can create stress or relaxation, pain or joy. The patterns and habits you have created through the years bring you to where you are today, to how you think, and the way you treat others. You know that it's hard to teach an old dog new tricks and, without question, understand that it's impossible to change events from the past. So, if it's hard to change your ways and even harder to rewrite history, what are you to do?

Change your perspective.

Change how you view both the past and the present, and commit to reframing your expectations of the future. Just as you use your brain to memorize facts, recall events, and process information, you can retool how you interpret events. You can recognize and stop unhelpful, judgmental, and negative thinking the moment it creeps into your thoughts. You can choose words that are affirming and supportive about yourself and others. Just as you can choose not to use bad or negative language, you can make the choice to not use destructive thought patterns to process what goes on in your life. Here are some positive thinking examples:

- Use "can" and eliminate "can't."

- Ask "How can I help?" as opposed to "What are you going to do about that?"

- Say good things to others and keep unsupportive, critical remarks to yourself.

- Focus on what is in your control—your behavior and actions—and forget about what you can't control—the behaviors and actions of others.

Stretch the possibilities by enriching your mind with positive, life-affirming thoughts that challenge your present way of thinking. Learn new ideas through reading, tapes, seminars, and classes. Stimulate your mind by experiencing new things. Go somewhere new for a short vacation. Take a nature walk and marvel in the majesty that surrounds you. Never get complacent. Keep growing and learning. Keep changing.

Just as your body needs nutritious food and exercise to stay fit, so too does your mind need to keep in shape. You will feel less stress and more peace of mind as you gain new information, learn new skills, and consider new ways of responding to both your private and professional happenings of the day. Just as software consistently improves, you can improve how you think. In matters of the mind, you are the programmer, and updated versions hold endless possibilities.

Reflecting on My Finding Peace

Private Point to Consider: The power of the mind is breathtaking.

Question to Myself: What do I have to do to create healthier thoughts and a more hopeful outlook?

Acts of the Mind

- Assess how much of your language is negative and unsupportive about yourself and others and how much is positive and affirming.
- Learn about alternative ways to view life and interpersonal communications.
- Keep changing and improving every day.
- Read a lot.
- Ask questions.
- Stay curious.
- Eliminate the word "can't" from your vocabulary.
- Question your assumptions.

My Acts of Mind

_____

_____

_____

_____

_____

_____

_____

_____

_____

_____

_____

Body

"Life itself is the proper binge."

—Julia Child

Be good to your body.

Little aches, pains, allergies, and the stresses of everyday life cause wear on your body. Your back, feet, and shoulders bear the brunt of your stress. Feeling stress and tension is distracting at best and tiring at worst. It takes you away from being relaxed and fully concentrating on the things that are important. Your body is like the engine of a car. You need to maintain your body and keep it in good condition to move forward. When your body is working as it should, you have the energy and strength to climb mountains.

There are many things you can do to be good to your body. Here are a few ideas:

Treat yourself to a massage and allow your tired muscles to be soothed, rubbed, and kneaded into submission. Take a bubble bath by candle light and relax. Try exercising. Taking a brisk walk is great and can be done almost anywhere. In the privacy of your home, exercise videos are great time-savers, as well as good ways to keep active. You save drive time if you work out at home. On the other hand, there are many who love the gym and the stimulation of having other people around. Do whatever works for you!

Another important way to enrich your body is through diet. Eating nutritionally sound, balanced meals adds energy and vitality to your day and helps eliminate excess poundage that has crept up on you over the years. Drink more water and less caffeine. Toss the sugary and fatty foods. Treat your body as you would your own baby, feeding it only good, wholesome foods.

Relax. Take time to wind down and put your feet up. Get a good night's sleep.

Accept your body for its uniqueness. No one has your same mouth, thighs, hair, or body shape. Come to terms with your roundness, thinness, color, and size. The sooner you cherish what can't be changed, the more content you'll be.

With a healthier, fitter, and more relaxed you, your body, mind, and spirit thrive in harmony. Don't take your body for granted. It is sacred—the temple that houses inner peace.

Reflecting on My Finding Peace

Private Point to Consider: Be good to your body.

Questions to Myself: What can I do to take better care of my body? What does my body need?

Acts of the Body

- Nurture your body.
- Treat your body like a temple.
- Eat well.
- Exercise.
- Drink plenty of water.
- Get a good night's sleep.
- Rest.
- Think positively.
- Be active.
- Learn to love the genetic gifts you have been given.

My Acts of Body

_____

_____

_____

_____

_____

_____

_____

_____

_____

_____

Time

"Time is lost when we have not lived a full
human life, time unenriched by experience,
creative endeavor, enjoyment, and suffering."
                              —Dietrich Bonhoeffer

Busy is the buzzword of the day.

Rushing. Squeezing one more thing in. You strive to get as much off your to-do list as is humanly possible. Yet, at the end of the day, how good do you feel? How satisfied are you with all that you accomplished?

I daresay you probably don't feel that great about all that you do in an average day. You're too tired to think about it. And there's always more to do tomorrow. In this never-ending state of rushing, you don't have time to breathe, let alone reflect or stay still long enough to give yourself a pat on the back for your hard work. But this isn't even the real issue.

There never seems to be enough time. With cell phones, email, fax machines, online shopping, and hourly calendars on which you even have to make an appointment to see your spouse, you are living in a constant time crunch.

The core of the matter is that it doesn't matter how efficient or productive you are. The more you do, the less you are. Peace is about being, not doing. It's about feeling, soaking in the moment, touching another person's life, making memories. This can't be measured in quantity of time. Quality is the yardstick—how you spend your time and how you share your soul.

Peace of mind has no place in this "do more" society. High blood pressure, headaches, and stress take over. It's time to take control of the clock and the precious gift of time that waits for no one. When you view each minute in the day as a fleeting opportunity to make a difference, touch a life, and be the best you can be, you heighten your sense of priorities and get rid of some of the nonsense around you. You spend time on what is important.

Start by making time for yourself. By saying "no" and giving yourself the permission to do only what you want to do and what is comfortable, you set essential personal boundaries to protect your spirit and soul. The need to please is replaced with a mindfulness that considers your personal priorities and weighs the value of the time expended to the quality of life produced.

Think about balance. Look at all of your responsibilities and priorities. Ask yourself, "So what if something takes two days instead of one, or if I do it next week instead of today? Or what if I don't do it at all? What's the worst that can happen?" Make time work for you and the good of your soul. Take time to be good to yourself.

Reflecting on My Finding Peace

Private Point to Consider: Busy is the buzzword of the day.

Question to Myself: How much do I value the seconds, minutes, and hours of each day by occupying my time with important and purposeful activities?

Acts of Time

- Manage others' expectations.
- Learn to say "no" to others and "yes" to yourself.
- Limit interruptions.
- Help your family to help themselves.
- Enlist support—don't do it all.
- Schedule personal time.
- When someone else can do it, delegate.
- Say "yes" to simplicity.
- Stop "shouldding."
- Work backwards, plan ahead.
- Take time to do nothing.
- Take time to rest and rejuvenate.

My Acts of Time

_____

_____

_____

_____

_____

_____

_____

_____

_____

_____

_____

Life

"What you are is God's gift to you; what you
do with yourself is your gift to God."

—Danish proverb

If you only had six months to live, how would you live your life?

How close are you today to where you would be if you lived your life like every minute counted?

The gap between the two is what needs to be filled in. You are only given this chance one time. To make the most of the precious gift of life, you need to live with purpose, love, and integrity. Take a moment to reflect on your life.

- What is good about it?
- What would you like to change?
- How can you do it?

You are in a unique spot in life in terms of finances, education, career, relationship, health, age, gender, religion, dreams, and abilities. But no matter what your current station in life is, when you set out to do your personal best and be the best person you can be, one foot in front of the other, head held high, hand outstretched to help another, and heart open wide, you should be proud. Listen to your heart.

By striving to be your personal best, making the most of every moment, and finding the good in all that happens, you more easily sail through the rough times. Things always have a way of falling into place. Life, by its very definition, is made up of good times and bad, ups and downs, highs and lows. You can fight it or ride with it. Remind yourself to go with the flow when things get a little crazy.

In the end, coming to terms with your life, its purpose and direction, and, most importantly, your ability to change its course, can only bring you closer to your dreams.

Reflecting on My Finding Peace

Private Point to Consider: If you only had six months to live, how would you live your life?

Question to Myself: What is my purpose in life—why I am here on Earth—and what do I have to do to fulfill my purpose with my unique gifts and talents?

Acts of Life

- Savor each moment.
- Appreciate the beauty around you.
- Be proud of who you are and your heritage.
- Show your family that you love them.
- Give to someone in need.
- Know that nothing lasts forever—the good times *or* the bad.
- Inject passion into every day.
- When in doubt, ask, "What would Jesus do?"
- Discover your purpose in life.
- Follow your heart.

My Acts of Life

_____

_____

_____

_____

_____

_____

_____

_____

_____

_____

_____

Security

"Man's security comes from within himself."

—Manly Hall

Security comes in knowing you are not alone.

As a child, security was knowing that things familiar to you were around: your parents, toys, friends, school, and home. As an adult, you seek the same security, albeit in a slightly different form. Your parents are replaced by your spouse. Your toys are replaced by your car, clothes, and jewelry. Your friends are replaced by your bank account. The security you seek is predominantly emotional, financial, and physical.

There is a security that comes with peace of mind that does not reside on the material plane. It is the inner knowing and confidence that you are safe and that things will work out for the best—that your dreams can come true. Faith is the key to feeling secure. It's not the size of your house, bank account, or security system that can comfort you. It's knowing that God is here, right beside you, seeing you through, lifting you up when you need a helping hand. You are never alone.

Faith comforts. Faith protects. Faith reassures. Faith consoles. Faith sees you through.

Reflecting on My Finding Peace

Private Point to Consider: Security comes in knowing that you are not alone.

Question to Myself: How can I renew my faith to know that God is with me?

Acts of Security

- Pray.
- Ask God for help.
- Talk to God.
- Learn that you are powerful and can move mountains.
- Trust yourself and your instincts.
- Be true to yourself.
- Visualize your dreams becoming reality.
- Know that this, too, shall pass.
- And, most of all, know that you are not alone.

My Acts of Security

_____

_____

_____

_____

_____

_____

_____

_____

_____

_____

_____

Crisis

"I like living. I have sometimes been wildly, despairingly, acutely miserable, wracked with sorrow, but through it all I still know quite certainly that just to be alive is a grand thing."

—Agatha Christie

Crisis is the unwanted fuel for remarkable, personal growth.

You open yourself to finding peace when you realize and accept that you will spend about 10 percent of your life feeling horrible. During these times, one crisis after another unexpectedly arises, your dreams are dashed, and your life is torn apart. Crying, screaming, ranting, raving, running, or hiding doesn't dull the pain. You wake up every day wishing you could just stay under the covers until the nightmare ends.

Sad to say, but it won't go away.

Crisis is a normal part of life. Lightning strikes a wooded area and thousands of acres are blackened. A hurricane touches down on land and devastates a region. An earthquake flattens a city and hundreds of lives are lost. What good comes of this horrific loss? Through the devastation, families come together, neighbors help one another, and strangers give money and shelter to help. You can find good in bad. Compassion. Generosity. Love. It's there—you only have to want to find it.

Crisis is a test of your will. You are forced to test your faith, patience, understanding, and forgiveness. Crisis generates change. Of course, no one generally likes too much change, especially when it comes in the form of bad news.

However, change is an inescapable part of life. The only thing you can do to adapt is to expect the unexpected. This means you have to stay flexible, ready to go with the flow and bend with the breeze. Like a supple reed that won't break in a howling wind, you must move with the forces facing you. Crisis is inevitable. Accepting and anticipating it helps you through. Loss in all its forms touches everyone. No one is immune. Know that you are not alone.

The key is to keep hope alive during crisis. Just when you think the clouds will never part, a rainbow appears and it turns into a sunny day. And so it goes in times of tragedy and loss. When you navigate the storm with faith and hope, knowing that the rainbow is sure to follow the rain, you can make it through and come out stronger, wiser, and more loving for having faced loss head on.

There are blessings in disguise in the greatest of tragedies. Seek to go beyond the dark days and bad times. Look for the light and the good.

Reflecting on My Finding Peace

Private Point to Consider: Crisis is the unwanted fuel for remarkable personal growth.

Question to Myself: How many crises have I been through and how have I successfully weathered the storms?

Acts of Crisis

- Keep the faith.
- Ride out the storm.
- Find the eye of the storm.
- Keep your head.
- Know that this, too, shall pass.
- Expect the unexpected.
- Find good in bad.
- Know that you are not alone.
- Be prepared.
- Remember the times you made it through other periods of great loss.
- Reach out to someone in need.
- Rise above the material loss and focus on the heavenly.

My Acts of Crisis

_____

_____

_____

_____

_____

_____

_____

_____

_____

_____

_____

Rights

"Don't compromise yourself.
You are all you've got."

—Janis Joplin

Rights are rules of conduct that keep your world safe and sane.

It is within your power to choose to say "no," to give permission, to change your mind, and to choose whether or not to use your power. You don't always have to please others or worry about being liked. You have the right to set boundaries and require that others treat you in a way that demonstrates respect and courtesy. People need to know how far they can go. In fact, sometimes you need to set limits just for yourself to remind yourself of the importance of personal dignity.

Often, we are our own worst enemies. We try to do too much and don't know how to say "no" assertively and let our needs be known. Think about your priorities and how you spend your time. Do what's important to you. Set boundaries when others take advantage of your good nature and ask you to do their job. Consider new ways to assertively let others know you don't agree and don't buy into what they want. Some examples are: "I understand how you feel. However, I am unable to do that. I hope you understand" and "I know this must be important or you wouldn't have asked me, but I can't do it, perhaps another time. Let me know in advance next time so I can build it into my schedule."

Rights are rules of conduct based on the values and morals that keep your world safe and sane. Set up your own personal bill of rights, like our Founding Fathers did. Let it be the basis of your constitution.

Reflecting on My Finding Peace

Private Point to Consider: Rights are rules of conduct that keep your world safe and sane.

Questions to Myself: How do I set personal boundaries based on that which is important and essential to my values, morals, and purpose in life?

Acts of Rights

- Set limits.
- Say "no" when you want to.
- Say "yes" to yourself.
- State your personal boundaries to others.
- Let others know when they cross your personal boundaries.
- Set consequences for transgressions.
- Develop communication tools that firmly, but gracefully, communicate "no."
- Prioritize the most important values and morals by which you want to live.
- Develop non-negotiable rights that represent the essence of who you are and how you want to live your life.
- Be an example of demonstrating your personal bill of rights in the way you treat other people.

My Acts of Rights

_____

_____

_____

_____

_____

_____

_____

_____

_____

_____

_____

The You of Tomorrow

A child dreams about the way life will be, imagining growing up, going to college, getting married, landing a great job, and having a household full of beautiful children. Then she spends the better half of her life trying to build the blocks to reach for the stars. She works, achieves, works some more, and achieves some more, until she finds her hair turning a little gray and her laugh lines deepening. Middle age creeps in.

In your dream quest, there is little breathing space for quiet moments to reflect on the fullness of your life, to appreciate all that you have.

Instead, you carry on, focused on all that you don't have yet. You're often in such a rush to get to the next place and reach the next goal that you miss the wonder of the moment and the beauty of the place you are standing in now.

It's a precarious balancing act—dreaming, trying to meet goals, moving, growing, and trying to keep hope alive for a better tomorrow while staying grounded in the reality that is before you and appreciating the many blessings you have. But it's not impossible. With your feet on the ground and your eyes on the stars, you can savor the moment and know that the possibilities are limitless.

Looking into the future can be so seductive. You escape into a world of your own, where fantasy becomes reality with all the love, money, health, and happiness you want. And dreaming is good, for how else can you achieve the impossible but to believe that the impossible is possible?

Hope makes all things possible.

You need hope and purpose in your life to muster the energy and motivation to carry on. Hope is your reason to live. I once saw a video about people who were subjected to the unimaginable cruelties of concentration camps and survived. These survivors, who were able to leave the camps against all odds and without having their spirits broken, shared a common bond of hope and purpose. One wanted to finish his research in medical science. Another found his purpose in reuniting and starting a family with his girlfriend, who had gone to the United States a year earlier. Another survivor wanted to complete a book she was writing. They all had a reason to live, something bigger than themselves—a purpose. They were able to keep hope alive—to believe in something invisible to the eye and foreign to the touch.

It is up to you to think about the future in a constructive, hopeful, and purposeful way in order to motivate and propel yourself forward.

This is easier said than done. Your fears and desires may sometimes get the better of you, like when that piece of rich chocolate cake calls your name and you succumb to the pleasure of the moment instead of remembering your goals of a slimmer you in the future. Know that some days you will be more far-sighted, hopeful, optimistic, confident, and sure-footed. Other days, you'll take one step forward and then stumble backwards. That's OK so long as you stay on your path and keep moving forward.

One of the greatest stumbling blocks is fear. Maybe it is fear of the unknown or fear of failure. Or perhaps it's fear of being loved because you think you're unworthy. Whatever the brand of fear, know that fighting your fears is instinctual, but facing your fears is inspirational. Just remember that you have to work on taming one dragon at a time or it becomes too overwhelming. Take a soulful introspection in the privacy of your world and honestly assess your fears. Face them head on. It's the only way to move forward.

Tomorrow offers unimaginable possibilities. You can do anything. You just have to believe. It is a mindset. Scores of the most successful people in the world were rejected time and time again before they got their first breaks. The successful ones believed in themselves, visualized realizing their dreams, and never gave up. That's the secret—never give up. Keep trying. To believe in yourself is to create endless possibilities.

In your journey of inner peace, keep close to your heart the knowledge that you can and will realize your dreams. Reach for the stars. Build your hopes of a limitless tomorrow with peace as your faithful friend guiding you toward the lessons from the past and create harmony and joy in every waking moment today.

Making Room

"The wisdom of life consists in
the elimination of nonessentials."
—Lin Yutang

Just as though it were time for spring cleaning, unclutter your life—out with the old and in with the new.

It doesn't matter what time of year it is. With snow on the ground or rain in the sky, there is no better season than the present to make room for peace today. Unload the old baggage, unfounded fears, and gnawing worries. Get rid of grudges, anger, jealousy, and old hurt. The hard-hearted need not enter.

Peace resides in a room with a view in the warm, safe, quiet corners of your mind. The view is of a blissful today with a backdrop of a brilliant and sunny tomorrow. It is a place where few reside and that many seek. Peace demands its own space in a place that only open hearts can build.

Reflecting on Finding Peace

Private Point to Consider: Just as though it were time for spring cleaning, unclutter your life—out with the old and in with the new.

Question to Myself: What importance do I give to simplifying my life in both my personal and professional worlds?

Acts of Making Room

- Set aside time to think and plan.
- Make achieving peace of mind a wondrous journey, not an end in itself.
- Enjoy the journey.
- Remember that forgiveness cleans up lots of messes.
- Make peace with the past.
- Count your blessings today.
- Savor the moment.

My Acts of Making Room

_____

_____

_____

_____

_____

_____

_____

_____

_____

_____

_____

Hope

"There is no medicine like hope, no
incentive so great, and no tonic so powerful
as expectation of something tomorrow."

—O.S. Marden

Hope is the nourishment that sustains your soul.

It gives you reason to live. Looking toward tomorrow with the confidence that everything you so deeply desire will happen, you are able to go forward with self-assuredness in all that you do and in all that you are.

Whether you are faced with an unfinished task, an unmet goal, an open relationship, a new job, or the promise of a new dream, hope gives you the energy to keep on. Renew your hope by taking some private reflective time to answer this question:

What will be your legacy?

Your legacy is the imprint you leave in the hearts and minds of those you have touched. Your legacy can be a relationship you have yet to develop or an important project you have to complete. Whatever is important to you, make your mark by consciously and faithfully following the path of the legacy you want to leave.

Hope is founded in faith—faith in God, and, above all else, faith in yourself, and your God-given gifts. Believing is a feeling of the spirit, something that can't be seen by the naked eye. It shines from within. Keep hope alive by keeping your faith in God and believing in yourself.

You can *do* anything you want to do.

You can *be* anything you want to be.

You are the *master of your soul*.

Reflecting on My Finding Peace

Private Point to Consider: Hope is the nourishment that sustains the soul.

Question to Myself: What do I have to do to be the master of my soul?

Acts of Hope

- Say "I will" instead of "maybe."
- Visualize the outcome of your efforts—in vivid shapes, colors, and sizes.
- Have faith in God.
- Have faith in yourself.
- Trust in God.
- Trust in yourself.
- Pray.
- Face your fears.
- Eliminate the word "can't."
- Define your legacy by the imprint you want to leave in the hearts and minds of those you touch, and do what it takes to make it happen.
- Remind yourself that rainbows are sure to follow the rain.
- Repeat: "I can. I can. I can."

My Acts of Hope

_____

_____

_____

_____

_____

_____

_____

_____

_____

_____

_____

Growth

"When I was a child, I talked like a child,
I thought like a child. When I became a
man, I put childish ways behind me."

—I Corinthians 13:11

One thing is certain: nothing stays the same.

Know in your heart that whatever troubles appear overwhelming today, they too shall pass. Faith and hope will see you through. Know in your heart that when you stop trying new things, fail to take chances, and avoid facing your fears, you stagnate. You stop growing. When you stop growing, you die—not necessarily in a mortal way, but in a spiritual way.

Make personal growth a priority. Don't get complacent with the status quo. Keep changing. Keep dreaming. Grow. Grow. Grow.

Reflecting on My Finding Peace

Private Point to Consider: One thing is certain: nothing stays the same.

Question to Myself: How do I face my fears?

Acts of Growth

- Take responsibility.
- Evolve.
- Try a new attitude.
- Face your fears.
- Do something different.

My Acts of Growth

_____

_____

_____

_____

_____

_____

_____

_____

_____

_____

_____

Change

"To keep our faces toward change and behave like free spirits in the presence of fate is strength undefeatable."

—Helen Keller

Life is for the living.

Everything that is alive is changing moment by moment. Leaves turn colors and fall, only to be reborn in the spring. The clouds cover the sky only to give way to the sun. Joy one moment is replaced by sorrow the next. Sicknesses are healed. The young age. When there is no change, there is no life.

Embrace life by welcoming change in every aspect of your being.

Reevaluate your assumptions.

Reassess your habits.

Question what feels safe.

Make fear your friend.

Set your spirit free.

Reflecting on My Finding Peace

Private Point to Consider: Life is for the living.

Question to Myself: Do I embrace change or do I fear it?

Acts of Change

- Be a chameleon.
- Try something different.
- React unexpectedly.
- Wear a new hat.
- Change your hairstyle.
- Make new friends.
- Take up a new sport.
- Eat a foreign food.
- Travel to an exotic place.
- Do a soulful self-inventory and question your habits.
- List what feels comfortable and safe in your life—then change it.

My Acts of Change

_____

_____

_____

_____

_____

_____

_____

_____

_____

_____

_____

Destiny

"Destiny is not a matter of chance, it is a matter of choice. It is not a thing to be waited for, it is a thing to be achieved."
—William Jennings Bryan

What is your destiny?

Some things in life are inevitable, out of our control, a matter of fate. That can be an intimidating thought to many. Most of us feel safe when we feel in control.

To be out of control, in the sense that you surrender to your destiny while making the wisest choices available, is a step toward finding peace of mind. The key is to understand that peace of mind comes when you control what you can, and, at the same time, have faith that your destiny will be fulfilled.

Each of us has a purpose for why we are here. Make wise choices based on love to shape the destiny that is yours and realize your life's purpose.

Reflecting on Finding Peace

Private Point to Consider: What is my destiny?

Questions to Myself: What am I doing to fulfill my destiny? What mountains are left to climb?

Acts of Destiny

- Surrender.
- Make wise choices.
- Have faith.
- Follow your heart.
- Reach for the stars.
- Keep your dreams alive.
- Know your purpose.

My Acts of Destiny

_____

_____

_____

_____

_____

_____

_____

_____

_____

_____

Choice

"I say if it's going to be done, let's do it. Let's not put it in the hands of fate. Let's not put it in the hands of someone who doesn't know me. I know me best. Then take a breath and go ahead."

—Anita Baker

The choice is yours. To make it a good day or a bad day. To share a smile or a tear. To give or to get.

The choice is yours.

You can live your life making excuses and rationalizations for all that you don't have, all that has been "done" to you, and all that you can't become, or you can choose to follow your heart, have faith in yourself and God, and believe that your dreams can come true.

The choice is yours.

By forgiving old hurts, learning from the past and, at the same time, fully living in the present, you are poised to make good choices.

When you view your life in terms of the choices you have made and have yet to make, you empower yourself to create a future of your making, based on personal choice. Give yourself room to make mistakes. Give yourself room to make your own choices and live the life you imagine.

Reflecting on My Finding Peace

Private Point to Consider: The choice is mine.

Questions to Myself: What kind of choices am I making toward being a better human being, fulfilling my purpose in life, and giving more than I get?

Acts of Choice

- Forgive the past.
- Live fully in the present.
- Make wise, loving choices for your future.
- Take personal responsibility for all that happens.
- Throw away excuses.
- Point fingers at no one.
- Don't worry about making mistakes.

My Acts of Choice

_____

_____

_____

_____

_____

_____

_____

_____

_____

_____

_____

Vision

"When I look into the future,
it's so bright it burns my eyes."

—Oprah Winfrey

Write your legacy and then live it.

Seeing is believing. Opening your mind to the possibilities—to what can be and to what you want—is a state of mind.

You see what you want to see.

You hear what you want to hear.

You understand what you want to understand.

See with your heart. The truth follows.

Reflecting on My Finding Peace

Private Point to Consider: Write your legacy and then live it.

Question to Myself: Am I following my heart toward achieving the goals I have set forth in my life?

Acts of Vision

- Know what you want—where you want to be.
- Have a plan.
- Follow your plan.
- Rechart your course as necessary.
- Reaffirm your confidence in tomorrow.
- Draw a detailed picture of how you want your life to look, feel, smell, and be.
- Write your legacy, and then live it.
- Imagine the impossible, and make it possible.
- See what is invisible to the naked eye.
- Follow your heart.

My Acts of Vision

_____

_____

_____

_____

_____

_____

_____

_____

_____

_____

Reason

"To have a reason to get up in the morning,
it is necessary to possess a guiding principle."

—Judith Guest

Ask yourself, "What is the purpose to my life? What is my reason for living?"

Once you have found the reason, live your life with your purpose in the forefront and your heart leading the way. You will find peace of mind to be your constant companion.

Reflecting on My Finding Peace

Private Point to Consider: What is my reason for living?

Question to Myself: What is my purpose in life and how can I fulfill that purpose?

Acts of Reason

- Find the meaning in all that you do.
- Look at your unique talents and God-given gifts and use them to help make the world a better place.
- Listen to your heart.
- Ask, "What is my reason for living?"

My Acts of Reason

_____

_____

_____

_____

_____

_____

_____

_____

_____

_____

Optimism

"Ah, but a man's reach should exceed his
grasp—or what's a heaven for?"

—Robert Browning

Wear a smile in your heart.

Reflecting on My Finding Peace

Private Point to Consider: Everything happens for a reason whose purpose becomes clear over time.

Question to Myself: Do I see problems as opportunities, obstacles as challenges, and losses as life lessons?

Acts of Optimism

- Smile instead of frown.
- Pray.
- Control what you can control. What's done is done.
- Know in your heart that this too shall pass.
- Make a "thankful list" for what you have, not what you don't possess.
- Count your life's blessings.

My Acts of Optimism

_____

_____

_____

_____

_____

_____

_____

_____

_____

_____

Empowerment

"One can never consent to creep
when one feels an impulse to soar."

—Helen Keller

Discard thoughts of being a victim, a pawn on life's chessboard.

We live in a power-oriented society. Everyone is trying to be in charge and in control. Although this can manifest itself in negative ways, there is a positive side to feeling powerful. Empowerment is the magic to believe that you have the inner power to be all that you want to be, to achieve all that you want to achieve—in short, to make your dreams come true.

Test the limits of your being, take control, and do what you think you cannot do.

Empowerment is taking control of your destiny, being responsible and accountable for your actions. No blame placed. No victims allowed. You will feel less stress when you feel empowered, take control, and make your own choices in the best way possible. A sense of empowerment is key to finding inner peace.

Reflecting on My Finding Peace

Private Point to Consider: Discard thoughts of being a victim, a pawn on life's chessboard.

Question to Myself: What can I do to take responsibility and make better choices to be in control of my own destiny?

Acts of Empowerment

- Take responsibility.
- Choose your own destiny.
- Make your choices known.
- Be accountable.
- Don't play the blame game.
- Take chances and revel in the consequences.
- Don't worry about pleasing others, just follow your heart.

My Acts of Empowerment

_____

_____

_____

_____

_____

_____

_____

_____

_____

_____

Confidence

"The hopeful man sees success where
others see failure, sunshine where
others see shadows and storm."

—O. S. Marden

Think "I can!" and you will!

It's all about perspective—how you see things. When you change the perspective from which you view an object, doesn't it appear to change? From one angle, the object appears large. From a more distant vantage point, it's tiny. When you change the perspective with which you view a situation, doesn't it make a difference? One person can interpret an event as devastating while another will see the same experience as fulfilling. The same holds true with regard to confidence—it's all in how you see yourself. No one can instill confidence in you. You must choose to possess it.

Your future is as bright as you make it. It is yet to be realized. Therefore, the images you create are yours and yours alone. Why not choose to take charge of the future with the confidence that all will turn out well and that your dreams will come true? Let anyone try to tell you otherwise.

Seeing is believing, and seeing with confidence is the surest step toward actualizing your dreams and realizing your goals. Doubt and insecurity create detours to keep you from feeling your personal best. Confidence and self-assuredness create a pathway to happiness and a sense of satisfaction.

The confident face their fears and try new things. The self-assured seek internal gratification and are less influenced by the approval and judgment of others. Clearly, confidence is a state of mind. Make a mindful choice to look up, not down, to dream big, not small, to live fully without folly.

Reflecting on My Finding Peace

Private Point to Consider: Think "I can!" and you will!

Question to Myself: How can I eliminate the word "can't" from my thoughts and vocabulary?

Acts of Confidence

- Eliminate the word "can't."
- Think about yourself in terms of all the wonderful qualities you have, not what you don't have.
- When you feel lacking, change the thing you think you are lacking into something you actively seek and try to obtain.
- Make the opinions of others not matter so much.
- Stay focused—you'll accomplish more.
- Practice what you want to become good at doing and being.
- Accentuate the positive instead of saying something negative when you feel "less than."
- Know that it's easier to think happy thoughts than sad ones.
- Be around people who make you feel good about yourself.
- Reassess your expectations and consider if they're too high.

My Acts of Confidence

_____

_____

_____

_____

_____

_____

_____

_____

_____

_____

_____

Knowing

"Where there is the tree of knowledge,
there is always paradise; so say the most
ancient and the most modern serpents."
—Friedrich Nietzche

Live your life knowing that peace of mind is a process, a blessed journey which only the wise wander.

Reflecting on My Finding Peace

Private Point to Consider: Seek to understand the purpose of your life.

Question to Myself: Do I take the time to understand why I am here on Earth and fulfill my purpose in life?

Acts of Knowing

- Expand your horizons.
- Gain new perspectives.
- Keep seeking knowledge.
- Enjoy the journey.
- Learn new things.
- Understand that peace is found in the moment and not in tomorrow.
- Make each day matter.
- Know that peace comes from within—you hold the key to unleash its power.
- Seek peace in stillness.

My Acts of Knowing

Compassion

"We cannot hold a torch to another's path
without brightening our own."

—Ben Sweetland

To be able to give to another human being what she needs is the greatest of gifts.

To simply give of your heart by seeking to understand and comfort is the mark of a generous spirit. To give of your material comfort to make another's discomfort disappear is a sign of compassion.

The ability to be human—to feel for someone in need and to do something about it—is a great gift. Compassion is a gift you can give yourself by opening your heart to the pain and hurt of another and filling the void with understanding, patience, generosity, and personal sacrifice. It is not often that people sacrifice and do without so someone else can have what is theirs. Know that the ultimate act of compassion is sacrifice. Be it setting aside doing things that are important to you so you can help someone in need or giving your last dollar to someone who has nothing, sacrifice is the stuff of heroes. It's a lot easier to give when you've got a lot.

Through acts of compassion, you help not only the one in need, but also yourself by the mere act of reaching out to a fellow human being. Healing takes its place in your heart and theirs.

Reflecting on My Finding Peace

Private Point to Consider: To be able to give to another human being what she needs is the greatest of gifts.

Question to Myself: How can I give without return to those in need?

Acts of Compassion

- Give of yourself—your time, understanding, and patience.
- Give of your possessions.
- Seek not to be understood, but to understand.
- Know, "There, but for the grace of God, go I."
- Forgive as you would like to be forgiven.
- Love as you would like to be loved.

My Acts of Compassion

_____

_____

_____

_____

_____

_____

_____

_____

_____

_____

Sharing

"Man should not consider his material
possessions his own, but common to all,
so as to share them without hesitation
when others are in need."

—St. Thomas Aquinas

All that you have is borrowed.

It is God's and you have the use of it for the time you are here. Know that whatever you have been blessed with will be multiplied when you share it with another.

When you give, you get. Not in the sense that you give in order to receive, but in the sense that by giving, you receive in return unexpected blessings and fortune. When you find that you are caught up in your own problems and fears, the best recourse you have is to distract yourself by reaching out to someone. When you turn your attention to other things, you forget about yourself. The more you do it, the more accustomed you become to it.

Other-directed living becomes a way of life. It can be addictive. It feels good to touch another's life with your heart and spirit, love, and even possessions. Remember that it always feels better to give than to receive. Share yourself with the world. You will be blessed tenfold.

Reflecting on My Finding Peace

Private Point to Consider: All that you have is borrowed.

Question to Myself: How can I make it a point to always ask, "How can I help?"

Acts of Sharing

- Give of what you've got.
- Reach out to someone in need.
- Ask, "How can I help?"
- Know that what you take for granted may be someone else's sweetest gift.

My Acts of Sharing

_____

_____

_____

_____

_____

_____

_____

_____

_____

_____

_____

Generosity

"'Twas her thinking of others
that made you think of her."
—Elizabeth Browning

Generosity of spirit is the greatest of gifts.

The size of the gift is not important. Rather, it is in the act of giving, particularly when it is a gift of the spirit, that you experience what it means to be generous. You give without thinking of how much it is costing you or what you will be left with. You give, pure of heart, and give abundantly. Peace, your most faithful and all-knowing companion, will quietly see you through, rejoicing in generosity as you reach out to those in need. To give without expectation of return is to show an uncommon kindness that only the generous of heart know well.

Reflecting on My Finding Peace

Private Point to Consider: Generosity of spirit is the greatest of gifts.

Question to Myself: How can I give without return?

Acts of Generosity

- Give what you have.
- Give what you want.
- Give what you lack.
- Give of your time.
- Lend a hand.
- Lend an ear.
- Give without return.

My Acts of Generosity

_____

_____

_____

_____

_____

_____

_____

_____

_____

_____

Some Final Thoughts on Peace

I hope that you find some peace, a little comfort, and a deeper understanding of yourself after reading this book. Though you may be going through tough times, feeling disappointed, hurt, angry, fearful, doubtful, or confused, know that this too shall pass. Most importantly, do two things: control what you can and find a support system to see you through.

I hope you consider this book a friend, a helpful partner in your support system that stays by your bedside. Pick up this book every now and then to reflect on the passages that resonate with you.

Above all, know that gaining a deeper sense of inner peace can only be discovered in the here and now. Today is the only place peace grows. In terms of the past, forgive to allow yourself to forget. The future is yet to be. The only thing you have to hold on to is today. Make each moment count. Create memories. Love your family and friends.

Hug a lot. Laugh a lot. Let yourself be loved. Give to the world the best you've got and the best will come to you.

And, above all, keep the faith.

God bless.

About the Author

Paula Peisner Coxe was born in Los Angeles and educated at the University of California, Los Angeles. She completed a master's degree in business administration at the University of Southern California. She lived in Spain for several years, is a management consultant and small business owner and is also the author of *Finding Time: Breathing Space for Women Who Do Too Much*. Paula lives and writes in Southern California with her husband and two daughters.

She would love to hear from you about any thoughts on the book, or questions you may have. Please contact her at:

Sourcebooks, Inc.

P.O. Box 4410

Naperville, IL 60567-4410